A History of Vermilion Corporation and Its Predecessors (1923-1989)

A History of Vermilion Corporation and Its Predecessors (1923-1989)

by
Frank A. Knapp, Jr.

Published by the Vermilion Corporation
Abbeville, Louisiana

Copyright © 1991
by the Vermilion Corporation
115 Tivoli St.
Abbeville, LA 70511-0027
ISBN 13 (paper): 978-1-935754-95-4

University of Louisiana at Lafayette Press
P.O. Box 40831
Lafayette, LA 70504-0831
http://ulpress.org

Printed on acid-free paper

CONTENTS

Acknowledgments vii

Introduction ix

Chapter I 1

Chapter II 6

Chapter III 25

Chapter IV 39

Chapter V 45

Chapter VI 55

Chapter VII 64

Chapter VIII 69

Chapter IX 73

Epilogue 78

Appendix A 81

Appendix B 83

ACKNOWLEDGMENTS

I express my sincere thanks to all living stockholders of Louisiana Furs, Inc., Louisiana Furs Corporation and their descendants who graciously supplied all the information available to them about the predecessor organizations to Vermilion Corporation. Their historical recollections filled many gaps in the period 1923-1957; and, in many instances, confirmed other source material or fragmentary materials. Even the lack of information on questions submitted to them was valuable in suggesting that no important source of data was overlooked in the search for historical materials.

I would like to single out two persons for their valuable contributions, without which the early predecessor years could not have been narrated with the accuracy and details as presented in the opening chapters. The late Clayton J. ('Pat') Adams, an officer and director of Furs, Inc. and Furs Corp. from 1934 until the dissolution of the latter in 1958, was familiar with the principals of these organizations and participated in the major decisions during these years. He not only provided detailed letters about his recollections but answered repeated inquiries and questions to supplement them.

Mrs. Dorothy Peterkin, widow of the late Dan Peterkin, Jr., provided invaluable documentary source material dating back to 1923, which her husband had apparently inherited from Joy and Sterling Morton, who had been central figures in Louisiana Coast Land Company, Louisiana Furs, Inc., and Louisiana Furs Corporation. These "primary sources" in combination with Pat Adams' recollections were the core for reconstructing and interpreting the history of the predecessor companies.

Finally, I am indebted to John P. Donohue for his discovery of factual errors, valuable observations on the early years of Vermilion's history, and materials on the chronological ownership of the landholdings, based on the abstract of deed conveyances.

Frank A. Knapp, Jr.

INTRODUCTION

Vermilion Corporation was organized and incorporated under the laws of Delaware in March 1958. It is the direct corporate descendant of five predecessor companies: Louisiana Land and Mining Company (1912), Louisiana Gulf Coast Club (1923), Louisiana Coast Land Company (1924), Louisiana Furs, Inc. (1927) and Louisiana Furs Corporation (1952). For brevity, these organizations will be referred to hereinafter without the Louisiana prefix and the suffixes (Company, Corporation and Incorporated) will be abbreviated or omitted.

The surviving descendants and certain business associates of the original stockholders of Coast Land and Furs, Inc., have provided a continuity of ownership, management, and composition of the boards of directors to the present time in Vermilion, although with an increasing variance from this pattern in the years since 1958, as will be outlined at the close of Chapter II.

Another unique feature, particularly applicable to the Gulf Coast Club and Coast Land and, to a lesser degree, to the three successor companies was the primary objective of the well-to-do persons interested in the Gulf Coast Club promotion who later invested in shares of Coast Land. They sought to enjoy the recreational hunting of migratory wildfowl from Canada and the north central states of the United States, other hunting and fishing sports, and to conserve the environment for this purpose.

In the course of time, the stockholders placed increasingly greater emphasis on the profit motive, recognizing the potential of the landholding for commercial development. In part this change was dictated by necessity after the bankruptcy of Coast Land in 1927 and the loss by the owners of over $1,200,000 in that era. In part, the change was determined by the board of directors' recognition after 1958 that an increasing percentage of Vermilion stockholders and stock outstanding was held by persons as an investment vehicle per se. These owners were either not hunters, had no access, or convenient and affordable access to this superb hunting habitat.

Until well into the Vermilion era, nevertheless, hunting seemed to be the priority for the well-to-do investors of the successor companies to Coast Land with conventional investment rewards of minor or of secondary importance. Most were enthusiastic, avid sportsmen, and high-ranking corporate executives and professionals who came from widely scattered parts of the country—Illinois, Louisiana, Missouri, Texas, Oklahoma,

Tennessee, New York, New Jersey, and other states. Ironically, the owners of Furs, Inc., Furs Corp. and Vermilion ultimately received excellent financial returns from their investments in the common stock in the form of overriding oil and gas royalty payments, the sale of royalty units, the exchange of Furs Corp. stock for shares in Humble Oil & Refining Company in 1958 and subsequently from dividends and price appreciation in the stock of Vermilion.

Another element of continuity in Vermilion's legacy is the landholding of about 125,000 acres assembled under a single ownership by 1923, approximately 70 percent of which is marsh, wetlands, bayous, canals, ponds, and natural drainage ditches. The land with its abundant natural produce of wildlife and fish and mineral production has been the principal asset of Vermilion and all the predecessor companies. It was held in fee simple from 1924 to 1958, when it became the 99-year leasehold of Vermilion without the mineral rights.

There is an old cliche about the three most important criteria in selecting real estate for investment purposes: The word "location" is repeated three times. This large tract offered a variety of nutritious natural grasses, seeds, water plants, and other vegetation which supported huge flocks of ducks and geese of many varieties during the fall and winter seasons. It is still considered a wildfowl "hunters' paradise," despite extensive commercial developments in the past five decades—on, near and offshore Vermilion Parish. The land is also the habitat of many species of native birds, furbearing animals, alligators, shrimp, fish, and crayfish. Beneath the surface, there were large reservoirs of oil and gas, first discovered and brought into production after 1940.

Finally, the location of the land generated other commercial income, particularly for Vermilion stockholders, such as land lease rentals, oil and gas pipeline easements, and surface damage payments from seismic operations from oil and gas service companies. In many years, these non-recurring revenues more than offset deficits from surface lease operations, such as trapping, cattle grazing, hunting lease rentals, fishing, and others. Obviously, most of these special commercial revenues are directly attributable to the development and expansion of the onshore and offshore oil and gas industry in the past five decades.

A brief word of explanation about the source material: Vermilion's corporate archives are relatively complete and comprehensive, reflecting the increasing complexities of operations and decisions, in comparison with the simplicity of the predecessor companies. Moreover, at least two directors and three directors emeritus, who participated in the early years of Vermilion's operations, have supplied "oral" history or verified certain facts and interpretations.

The corporate records of Coast Land, Furs, Inc. and Furs Corp. are either limited or scattered in unknown locations. Many of the gaps can be filled by drawing conclusions or making deductions from the documentary materials which are available. In any event, Furs, Inc., and Furs Corp. convened only brief annual meetings of stockholders and directors. Annual reports, minutes, financial statements, corporate correspondence and other records were probably succinct and of limited historical value.

On the other hand, descendants or relatives of the deceased owners of Coast Land and the surviving owners, descendants, other relatives, and business associates of Furs, Inc., and Furs Corp. have provided a wealth of accurate information on the operations of these companies in the form of documents, recollections from direct participation and oral history passed along by ancestors.

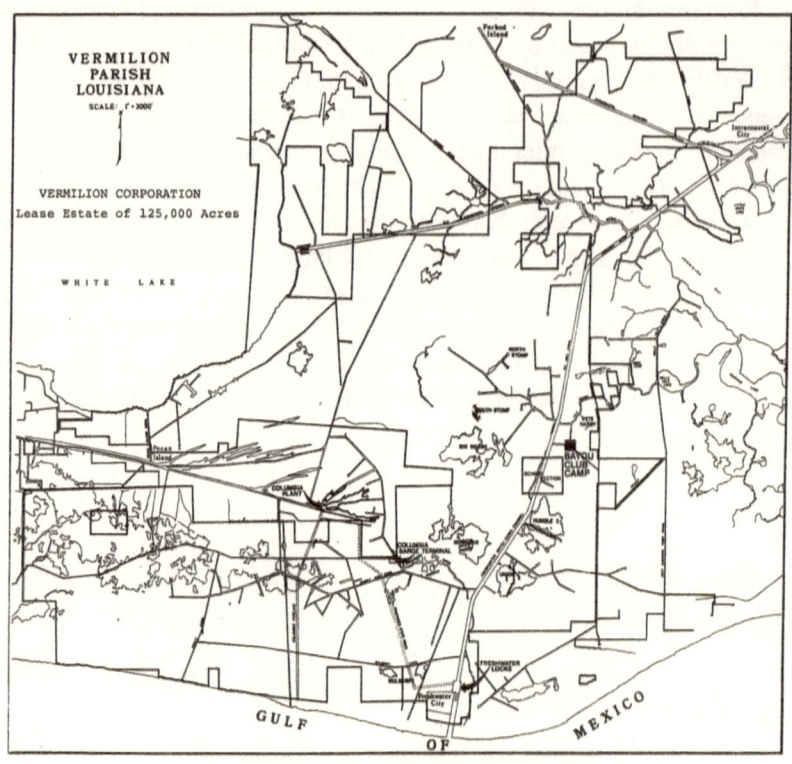

Vermilion Corporation's Lease Estate.

CHAPTER I

A BRIEF DESCRIPTION OF THE LEASEHOLD AND CHANGES SINCE 1923

The Vermilion leasehold is located in the west-central section of the Louisiana Gulf Coast within Vermilion Parish. The area is approximately 125,000 acres or about 190 square miles with external boundaries of somewhat irregular shape.

The southern boundary on the Gulf of Mexico is a twelve-mile stretch of narrow sandy beach. The eastern boundary (from north to south) runs from near the westernmost point of Vermilion Bay and follows closely the western boundary of the Rainey-McIlhenny & Louisiana Wildlife Refuge, now under the control of the National Audubon Society, due south to the gulf. The northern boundary (from east to west) begins near the westernmost point of Vermilion Bay and closely parallels Schooner Bayou a short distance north of this channel in a northwesterly direction to its juncture with the Intracoastal Waterway. It continues along the southern bank of this waterway in a west, southwesterly direction to the confluence with White Lake. The western boundary (from north to south) follows the indented and curving eastern shore of White Lake to the junction with the eastern boundary of the Rockefeller Wildlife Refuge and south along this boundary to the Gulf of Mexico.

Since this huge tract was acquired by the Louisiana Land and Mining Company and sold to Louisiana Coast Land Company in 1924, it has been held by Coast Land, Furs, Inc., and Furs Corp. in fee simple and by Vermilion as a 99-year leasehold with only minor changes in the boundaries and total area. Nevertheless, it should be noted that two documents prepared by knowledgeable sources variously describe the area as "over 100,000 acres" and "132,000." The first is a promotional brochure of the Gulf Coast Club (*America's Last Great Hunting Ground*, dated 1923), designed to attract the purchase of Club memberships by wealthy sportsmen. The second document is a pamphlet advertising the high quality of muskrat pelts prepared by Furs, Inc., dated 1938 (*Muskrats - their origin, habits and habitat*).

Some small acreage on the borders was subject to conflicting ownership claims and title disputes. These claims were either dropped or settled out of court with only two known exceptions. A claim of the state of Louisiana resulted in a court decision in favor of Furs, Inc., in 1938. In addition the state attempted to have the landholding re-surveyed by the Department of the Interior. This request was first denied by the Department in December 1930 and upheld by the assistant secretary of Interior in 1931.

On one occasion in 1928, the state also sold trapping leases on a portion it was claiming, but Furs management obtained a permanent court injunction against the lessees who did not contest the order. Another case was filed against Furs, Inc., over a title dispute involving several plaintiffs who were awarded about 500 acres of the landholding in 1939 under terms set forth by the Louisiana Supreme Court.

Bounded on the east and west by two wildlife refuges, the property had characteristics similar to these adjacent neighbors. In 1924, it was a *despoblado*, inhabited almost exclusively by great varieties of native birds, fur-bearing animals, deer, and alligators. The first category included waders, such as egrets, pelicans, herons, and gallinules, and many smaller species, such as terns, snipe, loons, quail, doves, and woodcocks. And from September through June, the huge flocks of ducks and geese of many species arrived from Canada and made the area a winter habitat or a feeding and way station before migration farther south. The marsh, shallow ponds, bayous and other waterways and the "high ground" produced an abundance of nutritious water plants and surface grasses, such as millet, blue tongue and alligator weed, adequate to support a dense wildfowl population.

The fur-bearing animals, also an abundant population, included muskrat—a major source of income for Furs, Inc., and Furs Corp.—mink, otters, raccoons, rabbits, and opossums. After 1940, the South American coypu, usually identified by the name of the fur produced or nutria, was introduced to the property by accident and multiplied rapidly. Nutria later replaced muskrat as the principal source of trapping income for Furs, Inc., and successor companies.

In the early 1920s, contrasting with later years, the sounds on the property were almost exclusively generated by the bird and other animal life and the waterways. Since the only access to the area was by marine transportation, the man-made sounds were from an occasional motor boat traversing the bayous or canals or the splash or oars from boats propelled by human energy. The nearest land connection to the property was an unfinished road which paralleled the Vermilion River from Abbeville south, terminating about seven miles north of the westernmost tip of Vermilion Bay, the easternmost point of the landholding.

Description of the Leasehold and Changes 3

Undoubtedly, the vast expanse of territory was invaded by poachers and other trespassers, and the air was pierced occasionally by the sounds of shotguns or rifles during hunting seasons.

In this era, the general tone, atmosphere, and coloring were those characterizing a natural wetlands wilderness and can be described with the alliteration of somber, subtle, and subdued. The water in the canals and bayous was a dark grey-green and the banks a brownish-grey, depending on sunlight or overcast weather and the time of day. The wildlife, some of which provided bright splashes of plumage, found natural camouflage in the surroundings.

In contrast to the relatively minor changes in the size and shape of the property after 1923, many striking man-made transformations have occurred on the surface. Most of these have taken place since 1935 and are primarily connected with oil or gas exploration and drilling onshore and later offshore Vermilion Parish. The major alterations were for the development of an improved marine and surface transportation "infrastructure."

After the initiation of onshore geological exploration and discovery and exploratory drilling after 1940, the dredging of canals accelerated greatly compared to the limited construction in prior years. These channels were essential to accommodate marine vessels of wider beam and draft to move heavy drilling equipment to the drilling sites and provided other logistical support for the completed wells. In time the property became laced with canals, opening a much more extensive access to all sectors of the property by water transportation.

By far the greatest change in the transportation infrastructure began with the decision of the U. S. Army Corps of Engineers to construct the Freshwater Bayou Canal across the central-eastern portion of the property from a cutoff of the Intracoastal Waterway a short distance west of Intracoastal City. The purpose was to provide public marine access to the Gulf of Mexico. This waterway now traverses almost 20 miles from entrance to exit. From north to south, it runs south-southwesterly for about ten miles to the Belle Isle Bayou outlet and then almost due south to the lock near the gulf coast. Except for the lock, the width is 125 feet and the depth 12 feet, reducing Vermilion acreage substantially and concomitantly increasing substantially the amount of water on the leasehold. The construction incorporates some sectors of bayous and private canals dredged at the time, including the namesake Fresh Water Bayou, Six-Mile Canal, and Belle Isle Canal. In breadth and depth, Freshwater Bayou Canal, when opened to traffic in 1968, was far larger than any of the existing canals and designed to handle large marine vessels and considerable traffic.

Vermilion Corp. made a concerted effort in 1959-1960 to influence the U. S. Corps of Engineers to select an alternate route (such as Vermilion Bay through Southwest Pass) for various reasons, with emphasis on the potential environmental and ecological damage to the surface and wildlife (see Chapter V). Unfortunately, this effort proved unsuccessful and the adverse effects forecast in 1959 largely materialized. Major salt water intrusion, heavy wave turbulence from traffic in the canal causing bank and levee erosion, the noise of the marine traffic disturbing the wildlife habitat and the loss of many acres to non-nutritious wire grass have become serious environmental problems causing heavy expenditures in an attempt to mitigate them.

Traffic in the Freshwater Bayou Canal has increased after 1970 somewhat in proportion to the development of offshore oil and gas fields which required frequent logistical support of large motor boats. The noise factor has been compounded by frequent flights of helicopters from Intracoastal City, crossing over or near the air space of the property at low levels, to offshore production and drilling platforms. These flights have apparently contributed to the reduction of migratory wildfowl and native bird species, particularly Canadian geese.

Although access to most sectors of the property is still via marine transport, Louisiana Highway 82 now traverses the northwest area around White Lake through Pecan Island south to the gulf and then west along the coast to Grand Chenier. Another all-weather state road, designed for hurricane evacuation, was completed across the property and opened to public transit in 1984. The northern terminus is near the small community of Pecan Island and crosses the leasehold in an easterly-southeasterly direction to a terminus at the Freshwater Bayou Canal lock on the Gulf of Mexico. This route has two bridges for crossing the Humble #1 and Mulberry Canal.

Two of the largest tracts of "high ground" are the locations of the settlement of Pecan Island, and the hunting, lodging, and other facilities at Belle Isle. The Pecan Island area in the north central sector of the property is on east-west ridge of varying width and height. In addition to the settlement, Columbia Gulf Transmission Company has constructed a gas dehydration plant on a 35-acre site, first leased from Vermilion-Humble in 1971.

Description of the Leasehold and Changes

The smaller area known as Belle Isle is in the central-eastern sector of the leasehold, located east of Freshwater Bayou Canal and about eleven miles south on the canal from the cutoff of the Intracoastal Waterway near Intracoastal City. Over a period of years, Furs, Inc., and successors have constructed a comfortable hunting lodge with two wings and dining facilities; an annex to the lodge for additional lodging capacity; and quarters and dining facilities for employees and part-time employees during the hunting seasons, such as guides and housekeeping personnel. These facilities have provided accommodations for the members of Bayou Corp. and their guests since 1958. The lodge and annex combined can accommodate about 40 persons at any one time.

Other major commercial installations on the leasehold provide logistical support for, or are facilities of, the oil and gas industry. Columbia Gulf Transmission Company also leases a 15-acre barge terminal site, located southeast of its gas dehydration plant, for storage and marine transport of condensate extracted at the latter. Exchange Oil Company also leases a 13-acre site for a gas dehydration plant north of the U. S. Corps of Engineers lock on Freshwater Bayou Canal.

In 1967, Rip Tide Investors, Inc., with headquarters in Abbeville, leased about 355 acres on the western bank of Freshwater Bayou Canal, adjoining and below the lock. This commercial marina venture is designated Freshwater City and provides logistical support for the offshore oil and gas industry, commercial fishing vessels, pleasure and other marine craft. Eventually, six marine slips will be constructed for docking, access to the area and other purposes. Freshwater City has its own road connection to the state route across the property.

Many of the commercial developements of the past five decades have caused considerable change to the surface of the leasehold, multiplied the human transit and accompanying man-made noises by a geometrical ratio, and reduced the natural wildlife population and areas of nutritious wildlife vegetation. Nevertheless, many sectors of the property still retain characteristics of an uninhabited wilderness applicable in the 1920s.

CHAPTER II

THE ORIGINS OF THE VERMILION LEASEHOLD, 1849-1927

The approximate 125,000 acre tract which today is the ninety-nine-year leasehold of Vermilion Corporation is essentially the same property deeded to the state of Louisiana in 1849 via the Department of State from public landholdings within Vermilion Parish, reduced by about 32,000 acres in subsequent title conveyances. The transfer was in accordance with the Swamp Land Act passed in the same year by the U. S. Congress, which contained the proviso that any proceeds from the sale or sales to third parties realized by the state had to be invested in swamp reclamation, levee construction, drainage, and other water and flood control projects.

In May 1883, the state of Louisiana sold approximately 157,060 acres of the tract deeded under the Swamp Land Act to Jabez B. Watkins for an unspecified consideration. Ten years later, he transferred title to the Orange Land Company, Ltd., a land development company with headquarters in Lake Charles, for a consideration of $1,400,000, reserving several sections on the perimeter over which he retained ownership. The size of the excluded sections is believed to have ranged from 32,000 to 47,000 acres of the original 157,060 acres. As president of Orange Land Company, Watkins may have held a majority or controlling interest in this organization.

In turn, Theodore A. Dees, a resident of Lake Charles, purchased the tract held by Orange Land Company in April 1923 for a consideration of $274,590.00, including the application of the $10,000.00 he had paid for a purchase option in December 1922. Under terms of the sale, the vendor agreed to pay the vendee $2.50 per acre if the estimated area proved to be fewer than "109,836 acres." One week later, Dees sold and transferred title to the property to Louisiana Land and Mining Company for a consideration of $549,180.00, including a cash payment of $74,590.00, and the assumption of Dees' outstanding $200,000 debt to Orange Land Company, the balance covered by two promissory notes with a principal of $137,295.00 each, maturing in two and three years, respectively. The tract was again estimated to be 109,836 acres.

Land and Mining had been incorporated under the laws of Louisiana in October 1912 with a "fixed capitalization" of $3,000.00 or 30 shares with a par value of $100.00 each. The original three shareholders also served as directors and officers: John Dymond, Jr. (28 shares), president; A. Giffen Levy (1 share), vice president; and E. Lloyd Posey (1 share), secretary-treasurer. With its principal place of business in New Orleans, the Company's major activities and objectives—as indicated by the name—were related to "all kinds of real estate" transactions, oil and gas exploration and drilling, and other mining operations.

Subsequent to this conveyance, E. A. McIlhenny, identified below, acquired nine parcels of land totaling about 221 acres in the Pecan Island sector from individual owners between the dates of May and August 1923 and sold these parcels to Land and Mining in June 1924. According to recollections passed down by officers and directors of Vermilion and the predecessor organizations, McIlhenny was believed to have a major or possible controlling interest in Land and Mining at this time, although there are no records of his share ownership. At the date of dissolution of the company in March 1937, W. H. McFadden, who played major roles as an investor, officer and director of the three predecessor corporations to Vermilion, was the "sole and only stockholder of said Louisiana Land and Mining," and self-appointed, non-judicial liquidator.[1]

In 1923, McIlhenny organized the Louisiana Gulf Coast Club, incorporated under the laws of Delaware, to promote a diversified and grandiose recreational and conservationist project, featuring hunting and fishing on the coastal property in combination with economic development. He inaugurated the financing of this undertaking in July with a press release in which he stated that his objective was to attract as many as "4,000 millionaires" as club members and investors.

* * *

E. A. McIlhenny was a central figure in the precursor era of Vermilion. He was an entrepreneur engaged in promoting land development, mining prospects, hunting, and other outdoor sports activities at Avery Island and nearby areas of the central Gulf Coast of Louisiana. A dedicated sportsman

---

[1] Records of the Corporation Division, Secretary of State, State of Louisiana. A. Giffen Levy, the original vice president of Land and Mining, arranged for publication of the notice of dissolution in the New Orleans press. Land and Mining apparently made no annual filings with the Corporations Division after filing the charter of incorporation. No records are available to explain the timing of McFadden's ownership of Land and Mining or his associations with the officers and directors.

and conservationist, he was also the president of the McIlhenny Company, maker of the famous Tabasco Brand Pepper Sauce, with headquarters and principal facilities at Avery Island.

He also circulated at this time a fully illustrated, thirty-five page brochure, entitled *America's Last Great Hunting Ground*, providing a detailed description of the varied species of wildlife and fresh and salt water fish on the property or in the nearby Gulf of Mexico. In addition to supplying tackle, boats, and other sporting equipment for club members, the Gulf Coast Club planned to build extensive lodging and recreational facilities and to develop canal and road transportation to and on the wilderness property. These included a main clubhouse in the central part of Pecan Island with modern accommodations and service facilities for 300 persons; two hunting camps capable of housing up to 35 persons each; an 18-hole golf course, swimming pool, and tennis courts; and riding stables, horses, and riding trails. Training novices in hunting, fishing, riding, and other sports activities, providing hunting and fishing guides and transportation services to and from the property and the Southern Pacific rail passenger station at New Iberia were also to be made available to club members.

The Club plan also comprehended the construction of "cottages" on the grounds near the main clubhouse for use of the families of members who wished to spend the entire winter season in the area. Alternatively, members who wanted to construct their own vacation-retirement homes in this sector of the property were to be granted long-term leases by the Club management for this purpose.

A second illustrated brochure entitled *Natural Resources and Land* (undated), prepared by the Gulf Coast Club and apparently mailed to potential clients at the same time, extolled the agricultural and mineral prospects of the property to be owned by future Gulf Coast Club members. The back cover of this six-page document featured a map of the land and surroundings, prophetically encircling producing oil and gas fields in nearby parishes—Lafayette, Jefferson, Acadia, and others.

E. A. McIlhenny is believed to have been the author or principal contributor to the two brochures which reflect his dedication to hunting, fishing and other outdoor sports and his unbounded optimism about the recreational and commercial potential of the property. However, his name is mentioned only once in the longer brochure in connection with the hunting of black bears on the Big Game Grounds near Avery Island, an area to be open to Club members and the proposed location of one of the two hunting camps.

Louisiana Gulf Coast Club

Natural Resources and Land Values

The principal objectives of the Gulf Coast Club were to develop a profitable recreational facility and to preserve the land and environment for hunting, fishing, and conventional activities associated with a country club. Closely related was the objective of wildlife conservation and promotion. The Gulf Coast Club planned to set aside a two-mile-wide strip, stretching from the eastern to western boundary, on which hunting would be prohibited. Management also proposed to increase the natural wildlife food vegetation on the property with artificial planting in order to increase the per acre wildlife population.

Although the directors and officers of the Gulf Coast Club reportedly were all Louisiana citizens, the advisory board of nineteen members, as listed in the longer brochure, had an office on Michigan Avenue in Chicago and were from various parts of the country, including a U. S. senator from Louisiana, John Dymond, Jr., two well-known authors and sportsmen, an associate editor of *National Geographic Magazine*, the editor of *Wild Life*, bank presidents and other top corporate executives.

The role of the advisory board was not defined in the brochure but presumably its major functions were to identify eligible wealthy sportsmen, provide lists to the Gulf Coast Club, and to solicit directly the purchase of memberships in the form of stock certificates. Only three members of the advisory board later purchased shares in Coast Land, the successor corporation to Gulf Coast Club.

The capitalization of the Gulf Coast Club was 4,000 shares—the target number of millionaires to be attracted to memberships as set forth in McIlhenny's press release—and the per share price was to be not less than $1,000 or minimum paid-in capital of $4,000,000.00. To qualify for club membership, an applicant had to own a minimum of one share of stock and also be approved by the Club's board of directors.

The Gulf Coast Club, which did not have title to the property, entered into a purchase contract in September 1923, with Land and Mining to purchase it for a price of $2,000,000. Of this total, $750,000 was to be in cash generated by the sale of the first 1,200 shares of the Club's stock. Chicago Title & Trust Co. was designated the recipient of the proceeds and custodian-payor to Land and Mining.

The Club abandoned the promotion in early 1924 and apparently became inactive at that time.[2] There is no evidence to indicate that any stock certificates were printed and sold.

---

[2] The Corporations Division, Secretary of State, State of Louisiana, records the date of withdrawal from operations in the state by the Gulf Coast Club, Inc. as December 1933.

Vermilion Leasehold, 1849-1927   11

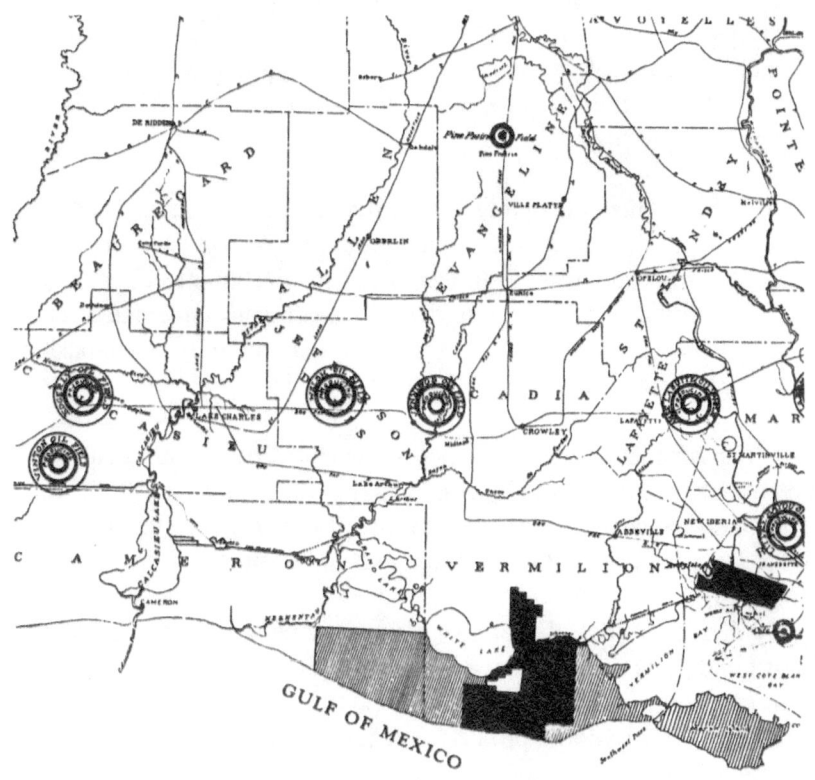

The club's property (102,000 acres) is shown in black.
The wildlife refuges are barred. Early producing
oilfields are indicated in circles.

The firm of Hay and Snyder of Chicago, acting as legal counsel for the successor Coast Land, made a search of the Club's corporate records but could not adequately explain its sudden disappearance from the scene. In a letter to the directors of Coast Land, dated August 7, 1925, the firm commented as follows:

> The last meeting of directors or stockholders of the Louisiana Gulf Coast Club, as shown by its minute book, was held on January 2, 1924, and aside from the usual organization meetings, and the qualifications of the securities of that company under the so-called 'Blue Sky Laws' of certain states, was the only other business transacted, as shown by the minute books.

In the same letter, with reference to the Gulf Coast Club's contract for purchase of the land from Land and Mining, the firm states: "... we assume that if the contract was executed that it was in some matter canceled so that Louisiana Coast Land Company could acquire title free from any prior claim."

By deduction from the number of wealthy persons who subscribed to Coast Land stock shortly thereafter—about 50—the Club promotion had fallen far short of the minimum subscription to enable it to proceed with the elaborate recreational project, as originally conceived, or even on a dramatically scaled-down plan. Moreover, those persons interested in the Club stock, if all subscribed, would have provided in total funds only a fraction of the contract price of the land.

The Club project was too grandiose and overly ambitious to be feasible, even with $2,000,000 of working capital after purchase of the property, the original Club goal. The cost of building the so-called infrastructure for the clubhouse and two hunting camps alone—sewage disposal, potable water supplies, electric and telephone lines, docking facilities, canal dredging, and road construction—would have been prohibitive. The same would apply to the cost of transporting workers, construction materials and equipment to the building sites via marine transport and providing temporary lodging and other support for workers during construction.

The Gulf Coast Club may have failed to meet its principal objectives but accomplished one major achievement in attracting about 50 or more wealthy persons, millionaires, and multimillionaires, to take a continuing interest in the land for recreational hunting and other sports activities and later for economic development. Undoubtedly with the endorsement of

E. A. McIlhenny and his support and cooperation, the group of recipients who apparently responded positively to the Gulf Coast Club's promotional materials organized the Coast Land Company and incorporated it under the laws of Delaware in April, 1924. The following month, Louisiana Coast Land entered into a contract with the Land and Mining Company to buy the same tract of land on the Louisiana Gulf Coast which the Gulf Coast Club had under contract for a purchase consideration of $2,000,000. However, the purchase price had been reduced by Land and Mining to $709,790.13.[3]

The charter for Coast Land emphasized land development and investment but also contained a provision for a hunting club. The capitalization was fixed at $1,000,000 with 500 shares authorized at a subscription price of $2,000 per share. Ownership of a minimum of five shares was required to obtain a club membership. The initial goal was to sell all five hundred shares and "to have 100 charter memberships. . ."

One year later—April 1925—this underwriting had fallen far short of the anticipated capitalization. The total subscription was $510,000 by 49 stockholders, but the actual paid-in receipts were $426,000 on the 255 shares then outstanding. Certain owners had given Coast Land promissory notes for a part of the balance due on their purchases, maturing between April 15, 1925, and April 15, 1926. The three largest stockholders, all of whom had paid in full for their shares, were W. H. McFadden, then a vice-president of Marland Oil Company located in Ponca City, Oklahoma (34 shares); E. W. Marland, president of Marland Oil Company (33 shares); and E. A. McIlhenny (20 shares). The rest of the owners held from one to five shares. (See Appendix A)[4]

The history of Coast Land, which spanned a period of more than three years, was a tale of constant financial crises, leading to the inevitable, terminal bankruptcy. The company was never able to free itself from in-

---

[3] McIlhenny represented Coast Land as its purchasing agent in this transaction. In the conveyance of the title, Land and Mining asserted that it was "selling the above property at cost."

[4] Even these results of the underwriting would probably not have been achieved, if the interested wealthy recipients of the Gulf Coast Club promotional materials had not shared these materials with friends in an attempt to solicit or invite their investments in Coast Land Company's stock. For example, Scott L. Probasco, Jr., now a director emeritus of Vermilion, has verified that his father was a good friend of the other two corporate executives resident in Chattanooga who also became original owners of Coast Land stock. McFadden undoubtedly solicited successfully the investment of E. W. Marland. And documentary evidence suggests that possibly several of the investors resident in Chicago were friends or acquaintances before the Gulf Coast Club promotion was undertaken.

debtedness; had no cash flow; and only "potential" sources of revenue, which required capital improvements on the property, such as dredging. The only source of raising new capital was the existing shareholder group, "since stockholders were unwilling to try to bring their friends in on this already shaky proposition."

Coast Land initially maintained two offices, one at the Chicago address on Michigan Avenue of the advisory board of the Gulf Coast Club and one at Avery Island, Louisiana, headquarters of the McIlhenny Company. In 1926, the Chicago office was changed to the residence of H. Collins Hay, then secretary-treasurer and a lawyer with the firm of Snyder & Hay in that city. The affairs of the company were to be managed "principally from the office in Louisiana and partly from the office in Chicago, Illinois," according to corporate records of the secretary of state of Illinois. In the required annual filing with the state of Illinois in February, 1926, the affairs of the company were then to be managed by the Chicago office but the principal place of business continued to be Avery Island.

The original officers and directors served only a brief organizational period. The replacements totalled eight directors, including two officers—Morgan J. Hammers, president and also president of the Nokol Company with headquarters in Chicago; and H. Collins Hay, mentioned above, as secretary-treasurer. All served until the demise of Coast Land in the fall of 1927. Three of the directors and their descendants were to play key roles in Furs, Inc., Furs Corp. and Vermilion: Joy Morton, president of Morton Salt Co.; Edwin H. Steedman, president of Curtis Manufacturing Company of St. Louis; and Scott Probasco, president of American Banking & Trust Company of Chattanooga.

Closely related to the Company's recurring financial crises was the apparent lack of control over finances, expenditures, and financial records from the two distant offices. An example is a filing by Coast Land with the state of Illinois, before the certificate of authority was voided in November 1926, for "failure to pay the franchise tax." The secretary-treasurer listed the assets of Coast Land in a totally indecipherable manner: Machinery & Real Estate, $960,098.25; Organization Expense, $29,082.68; Book Accounts and Notes, $71,479.33; Cash in Bank, $5,344.46; and two other items totalling about $2,000. The value of all assets held in Illinois was listed as a bank account with a balance of $143.39.

The beginning of the continuing financial crises of Coast Land was almost immediately after its incorporation in 1924 and after it executed its contract to buy the property from Land and Mining for $709,790. The paid-in capital for the shares purchased was only $510,000, assuming full collection of the promissory notes outstanding. To meet the balance owing to Land and Mining to gain clear title to the land, management obtained a loan from W. H. McFadden in the form of first-lien notes in the amount of $407,000, maturing in the fall of 1925.

Management then exercised the one alternative apparently open to raise additional capital—the sale of a bond issue to those stockholders willing to risk more funds in the enterprise. With such a minuscule potential market, it was obviously extremely difficult and hazardous to obtain an underwriter for this senior security of a size to cover the payment of the notes outstanding.

A prospectus was issued in June 1925 on a $450,000 maturity of "First Mortgage Bonds," with the Hibernia Bank & Trust Company of New Orleans acting as "trustee" and the underwriter. A total of 26 stockholders of Coast Land subscribed to $315,000 of the bonds. Hibernia Bank then loaned a "syndicate," the composition of which is unknown, the funds to buy the under subscription.

By far the largest subscriber to the bond issue was Joy Morton ($45,000) and four other persons each subscribing $25,000 were next in rank, including McFadden and Steedman. E. W. Marland and E. A. McIlhenny, two of the largest stockholders of Coast Land, did not subscribe to the offering. The proceeds were used to retire the first lien notes held by McFadden.

In retrospect and in light of the purchasing power of the sums invested in stock and bonds in that era, an explanation of the risk of the additional capital in bonds seems plausible only from a comment in corporate records related to the circulation of the prospectus: "Everyone associated with the Land Company expressed the belief that various capital improvements, principally a system of canals, would result in large earning power."

The proceeds from the bond issue provided only a brief pause in the rapidly deteriorating financial condition of Coast Land. In early 1926, another syndicate of stockholders was organized to raise cash to meet overdue debts estimated at $47,000. The sum was raised by March from the sale of promissory notes ("trustee loans") to twelve stock and bondholders. Again, the largest lender was Joy Morton in the amount of $9,250.00.

During the remaining months of 1926 and until the sheriff of Vermilion Parish foreclosed the property in mid-1927, various desperation efforts were made to raise new capital in order to meet overdue obligations and for working capital purposes. The amounts varied from $270,000 to

$400,000. The only additional capital which could be raised, however, was $16,750 in obligations denominated "receivor certificates," loaned by six bondholders with Joy Morton continuing as the largest lender in the amount of $6,200. Meanwhile, overdue bills went unpaid and provoked threats of lawsuits, including a $37,325 claim of Snyder & Hay for legal services and advances and a canal dredging bill of over $4,000.

Coast Land then began the preparation of an elaborate plan of reorganization ("Basis of Assessment and Exchange of Securities under Proposed Reorganization") which was never implemented. Under the terms of this plan, the bondholders would exchange 50 percent of the maturity value of their subscriptions for new common shares to be issued and holders of the trustee loans and receivor certificates would make the exchange for the new issue common at 100 percent of the maturity value of their senior debt issues.

Owners were also expected to purchase additional shares to meet expenses and to provide working capital for the reorganized company in the amount of $105,000 in addition to the purchase of $109,000 of the new issue shares under a "Special Assessment to meet the payment of a $109,000 note," on a pro rata basis to their senior security holdings. Apparently, the holders of the original common shares of Coast Land were to receive nothing or have to accept a major dilution of their holdings.

Acting independently of management after late 1926 through April 1927, "the Bondholder Protective Committee," organized for obvious reasons, was seeking to raise money from the bondholders to pay expenses of a foreclosure sale, obtain title to the land again, and working capital to operate profitably a newly organized company.

After Hibernia Bank & Trust intervened with a foreclosure suit, filed in the U. S. District Court, Western District of Louisiana, in June 1927, the First Mortgage Bondholders hastily organized a "syndicate" to bid for purchase of the property. "Almost all bondholders" participated in the subscription of a total of $258,000.00.

Since Coast Land did not meet the ten-day deadline notice for payment of principal and interest owing on the First Mortgage Bonds, it was legally declared in default, the property foreclosed, and a Special Master appointed by the court to conduct the sale. He advertised the public auction in July with advance notice that the minimum acceptable bid would be $200,000.00.

The sale was held on August 20, with the bondholder syndicate submitting the wining and only bid at the auction. E. H. Steedman, of St.

Louis, G. F. Meehan of Chattanooga, and Morgan J. Hammers of Chicago, all being major investors in Coast Land, acted as trustee-representatives for the syndicate. In late November, they filed a petition with the Special Master verifying that their purpose in the purchase of the foreclosed property was to vest title in a corporation to be organized under the laws of Delaware with the name Louisiana Furs, Inc. With the delivery of the First Mortgage Bonds and coupons and payment of the $200,000, the Special Master confirmed the title and transferred the deed.[5]

In this manner, the participating members of the bondholders syndicate became the original stockholders of Louisiana Furs, Inc., apparently with $58,000 of working capital before deducting legal costs of the land transaction—a contrast to the indebtedness of Coast Land from the outset of its operations. At that time, the owners of stock and senior securities of Coast Land and subscribers to the land purchase syndicate had invested a total of about $1,450,000 to purchase and regain title to the property.

During the more than three-year period of active operations of Coast Land, the officers, directors, and stockholders had to concentrate their efforts fully on coping with financial turmoil and survival, raising additional capital, and legal problems. The primary objective of most stockholders was to enjoy hunting, fishing, and other recreational activities and to build facilities and acquire equipment for these purposes, "luxuries" the investors could not afford without investment capital.

A few stockholders visited the property and some apparently participated in hunting during the seasons. At least plans were formulated to accommodate up to 25 persons "in comfortable temporary quarters" for hunting migratory wildfowl during the 1924 season. And an "Estimated Schedule of Necessary Expenditures During Winter of 1924-25" was compiled, including a water well and tank, miles of canal dredging to be completed, boats, trucks, fixtures for "eleven bathrooms" and "additions to house at Avery Island." The total estimated amount for all items listed was $75,675.

As a result of the experiences of Coast Land, the owners of Furs, Inc. were prepared to place emphasis on profitable sources of revenue from the property in order to generate funds for working capital, to build comfortable facilities on it, and acquire marine and other specialized equipment. In fact, an important legacy of Coast Land was to identify some of the potential

---

[5] Furs, Inc. did not obtain a Quitclaim Deed from Land and Mining until February 1937 "at a cost of about $100.00."

sources of revenue which continue today to be important income operations for Vermilion—hunting leases, trapping shares, cattle grazing fees (cattle raising was also considered), and farming.

W. H. McFadden also recognized the oil and gas potential at an early stage, obtaining a mineral lease on all but 30,000 acres of the entire tract from Coast Land for an unknown consideration, possibly a partial compensation for his loan of $407,000. He was later to purchase mineral rights on all but 30,000 acres of Furs, Inc., property shortly after it was incorporated in late 1927.

R. C. Vilas, a stockholder of Coast Land and resident of Chicago, presented what appears to have been a representative view of the primary original investment objective and the change toward an increasing awareness of the potential of the land for economic development with a profit motive. After an extensive orientation visit to the property lasting several days, he addressed a detailed letter to another stockholder, dated June 23, 1924, describing in glowing terms the agricultural, grazing, and trapping prospects of the land:

> When I subscribed for two full underwritings in the Louisiana Coast Land Company [four shares at a cost of $8,000], I had in mind only the desire to join a club from a hunting, fishing and general 'outdoor Southern winter sports' standpoint, and gave very little thought to the commercial and investment possibilities that might develop, and I think most of my fellow associates in this enterprise looked at the matter in the same way.
>
> There is no doubt but that on our 132,000 acres of high land and marsh land, we will have the finest duck, goose, quail, dove and big game hunting that can be found in this country, and aside from this wonderful hunting, the deep water fishing along the coast of Louisiana is probably as fine as anywhere on the continent. Most of us have probably heard these remarks before regarding hunting and fishing . . . but what most of us, including myself, did not know about, or think much about is the large commercial possibilities of the proposition. . . . . . . [6]

---

[6] Vilas included in this acreage figure the so-called Big Game Hunting Grounds for black bear and deer, a forested area to which members of the *Gulf Coast Club* were to have exclusive hunting rights, not title to the land. This approximate 20,000 acres adjacent to Avery Island belonged to members of the McIlhenny family and were not included in Coast Land property.

Vermilion Leasehold, 1849-1927

After mentioning canal dredging and road construction projected for the property or near it, Vilas concluded:

> I see no reason why we should not receive in the course of three or four years a net income from the natural resources of the property of at least $200,000.00 a year, which would be 20% of our capital, and I am firmly of the opinion that within the next three or four years, the present stock in Louisiana Coast Land Company will be worth many times what we paid for it from strictly a commercial standpoint, not to mention the increased value as a hunting and fishing club, for the game in this country, we all know, is getting scarcer every year, but on our lands the game will multiply rapidly with the care and protection that we will give it.

* * *

Perhaps the most important legacy of Coast Land, mentioned earlier in this chapter, was the establishment of a continuity of officers, directors and stockholders—through descendants, other relatives and business associates—to the present time in all three successor corporations, Furs, Inc., Furs Corp., and Vermilion. The identification of some of the prominent families, descendants, and business associates at this stage is designed to clarify the ties, connections, and roles of personalities to be mentioned in later chapters and to serve as a convenient reference.

I. *The Morton Family and Associates*: Joy Morton, president of Morton Salt Company, had invested the largest sums in the senior securities of Coast Land at the time of its dissolution and served as a director. He was elected president and a director of Furs, Inc. when it was organized and incorporated in late 1927. Sterling Morton, who succeeded his father as president of Morton Salt Company at the time of the latter's death in 1934, was also chosen to replace his father as president of Furs, Inc. in May of that year and served in that capacity and as a director until 1952 and with the successor Furs Corp. from 1952 until its dissolution in 1958.

Clayton J. ("Pat") Adams, an associate and assistant to Sterling Morton, served as a vice president, secretary-treasurer and director of Furs, Inc., from 1934 to 1952 and continued in all but the secretarial capacity

Annual meeting of the board of directors,
Louisiana Furs, Inc., at Belle Isle, La., in November 1951.
Seated, left to right: Richard Baldwin, Clayton J. Adams,
W. H. McFadden, Sterling Morton, Scott Probasco, and Dave Wallace.

with Furs Corp. until its dissolution. He and Lloyd McBride were principals in implementing the acquisition by Humble Oil & Refining Company (hereinafter referred to as Humble Oil) of Furs Corp. in 1958 and the organization and incorporation of Vermilion and the not-for-profit Bayou Corporation, a recreational hunting club. Adams is generally given major credit for negotiating the retention of the 99-year surface lease of Vermilion as an integral part of the terms of the Humble acquisition of Furs Corp.

Adams also served from 1958 until his retirement in December 1980 as a director and member of the Executive Committee of Vermilion. He and three other Directors who retired some years later—Edmund McIlhenny, Sr., Scott L. Probasco, Jr., and George Westfeldt, Jr.—continue their association with the board as directors emeritus.[7]

Lloyd M. McBride, senior partner in the Chicago law firm of McBride, Baker, Wienke & Schlosser (later McBride & Baker), was Sterling Morton's attorney and also provided outside legal counsel from time to time for the Morton Salt Company. He presumably obtained shares in Furs Corp. through these professional associations. As noted, he played a key role in the Humble acquisition of Furs Corp. and also in the organization of Vermilion and Bayou.

McBride served as general counsel of Furs Corp. and also as secretary. He was the secretary and general counsel of Vermilion from 1958 until his death in December 1983 and was one of the original directors. From 1980 until 1983, he was also a member of the Executive Committee.

Daniel Peterkin, Jr., president of Morton Salt Company and later chairman and president of Morton-Norwich Corporation, was a shareholder of Furs, Inc., and Furs Corp. apparently through this corporate connection and association with the Morton family. He inherited these shares from his father who preceeded him as president of Morton Salt Company. He served as a director and senior vice president of Vermilion from 1958 until his death in May 1988. He was the last active director with tenure dating back to the founding of Vermilion.

Garfield King, the treasurer of Morton Salt, was another Morton associate who was a stockholder of Furs, Inc., Furs Corp., and later Vermilion.

II. *The Steedman and Baldwin Families*: Edwin H. Steedman, the president and a major stockholder of Curtis Manufacturing Company of St. Louis (a diversified manufacturer of industrial products) was a dedi-

---

[7] Pat Adams died in February 1990.

cated sportsman with interests ranging from hunting and fishing to yacht racing. He was the second largest investor in the senior securities of Coast Land and a director at the time of its dissolution. Richard Baldwin, his son-in-law, was a director of Furs, Inc. and Furs Corp. and the first and only president of Vermilion until his death in November 1980. Edwin S. Baldwin, a son and partner in the St. Louis firm of Armstrong, Teasdale et al., has served as a director since 1980. Several descendants of E. H. Steedman and Richard Baldwin are stockholders of Vermilion.

III. *The Probasco Family*: Scott L. Probasco, the president of American Banking and Trust Co. of Chattanooga, became a director of Coast Land shortly after its incorporation. He also served in this capacity with Furs, Inc., Furs Corp., and with Vermilion from 1958 until his death in 1959. Scott L. Probasco, Jr. served as a director of Vermilion from November 1959 until his retirement in December 1985. He is currently the chairman of American National Bank and Trust Company in Chattanooga. Several members of the Probasco family are Vermilion stockholders.

IV. *The McIlhenny Family*: E. A. McIlhenny did not subscribe to stock in Furs, Inc., perhaps because he did not invest in the First Mortgage Bonds of Coast Land. Apparently, only the syndicate of bondholders who invested money to repurchase the land at the auction sale in Abbeville in August 1927, had access to the initial tender of shares by the successor Furs, Inc.

The McIlhenny family connection was reestablished in 1959, when Edmund McIlhenny, Sr., a partner with the New Orleans law firm of Chaffe, McCall, Phillips et al., accepted the position of Louisiana Legal Counsel with Vermilion. From 1962 until his retirement in December 1986, he also served as a director, member of the Executive Committee and, after 1964, as a member of the Land Management Committee.

Edmund McIlhenny, Jr., vice president of the McIlhenny Company, has served as a director since mid-1985 and also as a member of the Executive Committee and Land Management Committee since December 1986. He assumed the additional duties of vice president and secretary in December 1988. Other family members and relatives who have served on the Board of Vermilion are Walter McIlhenny, president of the McIlhenny Company, from December 1980 until his death in June 1985; and George Westfeldt, Jr., president of Westfeldt Brothers, Inc., of New Orleans, from December 1980 until his retirement in December 1986.

V. *The McFadden Family*: As noted earlier, W. H. McFadden, was the vice president of Marland Oil Company with headquarters in Ponca City,

Oklahoma, when he subscribed to the stock of Coast Land. He later became the chairman and principal stockholder of Southland Royalty Company which moved its headquarters from Ponca City to Ft. Worth, Texas, in 1938. He served as a director and vice president of Furs, Inc. and Furs Corp. until his death in 1956. Although he had no lineal heirs, his widow had relatives who are—or were—Vermilion stockholders. McFadden was the largest investor in Coast Land securities, common stock and bonds combined.

McFadden sold an unknown number of shares of Furs, Inc., to employees of Southland Royalty. Frank A. Knapp, Sr., one of the buyers, became in later years a director and vice president of Southland Royalty Company. He served as a director and member of the Executive Committee of Vermilion from 1958 until his death in December 1963. Frank A. Knapp, Jr., has served as a director since December 1964 and as president of Vermilion from December 1980 to December 1988, when he was elected chairman. Anna J. Ludlum, McFadden's personal assistant and secretary, now deceased, was a stockholder in Vermilion and the two predecessor companies and her son is now a stockholder of Vermilion. In addition, several former employees of Southland Royalty Company and descendants of former employees were Vermilion stockholders at the close of 1989.

VI. *The Watkins Family*: Horton Watkins, president of the International Shoe Company of St. Louis, was one of the largest investors in the stock and senior securities of Coast Land. His descendants today maintain their ownership of Vermilion stock.

VII. *The Miller and Kibbe Families*: Two Louisiana residents, prominent in their respective professional careers, acquired shares in Furs, Inc., probably shortly after its organization in 1927. Their interest in this investment is readily understandable by the circumstances and deductions, although there is no written or hearsay evidence available of the details of purchase. Both were stockholders of Vermilion at the time of death, and a number of descendants of each family continue their ownership of Vermilion stock.

Dr. Martin O. Miller, a physician practicing in New Orleans, owned land adjacent to or near Furs' property. He and his descendants grazed cattle herds on the landholding of Furs, Inc., and Furs Corp. and later on the Vermilion leasehold from 1937 until 1978. Miller had a close friendship with J. Mark Hebert, the supervisor of Furs, Inc., operations from 1928 until the mid-1940s when he became resident manager. Dr. Miller was probably acquainted with a number of other officers and directors of Furs, Inc.

J. E. Kibbe, an attorney with law offices in Abbeville, also apparently had the opportunity to purchase shares in Furs, Inc., through his acquaintance with officers and directors and possibly from legal counsel he may have provided the corporation from time to time. Kibbe was elected the first assistant secretary of Vermilion in 1958. A large number of his descendants retain their ownership of Vermilion shares.

There is no evidence available to explain how other top-ranking corporate executives became investors in Furs, Inc., and Furs Corp. stock. To list a few: Dave Wallace, a senior vice president of Chrysler, served as a director and vice president of Furs, Inc., and Furs Corp. until 1958; as a Director of Vermilion from 1958 to 1962; and as the first president of Bayou Corporation. George A. Lyon, Sr., president and owner of a firm manufacturing auto parts located in Detroit, was a stockholder of Furs, Inc. and Furs, Corp. His son, George A. Lyon, Jr., served as a director of Vermilion from 1958 to 1962. Harlow Curtice, chairman of General Motors, was a stockholder of Furs Corp., possibly of Furs, Inc. and also of Vermilion at the time of his death. The executors of the estate liquidated the holdings in 1964.

CHAPTER III

THE ERA OF FURS, INC., AND FURS CORP., 1927-1958

The defunct Coast Land Co. was reorganized within a few weeks after the repurchase of the land and incorporated under the laws of Delaware in late October 1927 to engage in the marketing and trapping of fur pelts. Two names were under consideration for the new corporation—Louisiana Furs, Inc., and Vermilion. The former was selected at the suggestion of Dr. R. O. Young, the newly appointed resident manager - director. He explained to the other directors that the latter name "would probably be a mistake because of the local superstition that any firm with the name 'Vermilion' would be unsuccessful."

The initial capitalization was an authorized 7,500 shares and offered to the small eligible market at purchase price of $100 per share or the same amount as the par value. Sixty percent of this amount had been paid in advance on an unknown number of shares, presumably by members of the former bondholder syndicate of Coast Land.[1] The balance "pledged" by them was called in for payment immediately. The company then purchased the moveables on the property, probably small boats, hunting and other equipment, at an auction sale for less than $1,900.00.

During organizational proceedings, the officers elected in addition to Young were Joy Morton, president; W. H. McFadden, vice president; and Morgan Hammers (former president of Coast Land), secretary.[2] The fifth director elected was Scott Probasco. Apparently on the recommendation of Young, management also appointed J. Mark Hebert to the position of supervisor of daily operations. Around 1944, he replaced Young as resident manager.

---

[1] On a Furs Inc. filing, dated December 1951, the Corporation Division of the secretary of state of Delaware made a manuscript alteration of the date of incorporation from November 10 to October 31, 1927. This same document has entries of 7,500 shares authorized and 7,500 issued. "Issued" does not equate to "outstanding," since only 5,122 shares were outstanding at that time.

[2] According to C. J. Adams, Hammers had a tendency to be verbose "and included in the minutes extraneous matters which had nothing to do with the business of the meetings."

Young was a physician residing in Youngsville a few miles northeast of Abbeville. He had provided services to Coast Land in the final days of its operations and reportedly sought a full-time position with the reorganized company. He requested an exchange of his unpaid fee of $5,000 owing from Coast Land for 50 shares of Furs stock and the certificate was finally issued to him at the close of 1931. In the advertising brochure entitled *Muskrats*, Young is described as follows:

> The direct management of this business is in the capable hands of five men who comprise the Board of Directors. The active management rests with the managing director, who has an outstanding record as a plantation manager, agriculturalist and executive.

The administration, management, and surface operations of Furs, Inc., and later Furs Corp. share certain similarities with those of Vermilion today, although the latter's revenues are much larger and its operations are far more complex than its predecessors. Like Vermilion, Furs, Inc., established two offices, the "upland headquarters" in Youngsville and the administrative headquarters in Chicago, the executive office of Joy Morton in the headquarters of the Morton Salt Company on South La Salle Street. Furs Corp. and later Vermilion maintained this pattern until 1984, but with a change of the Louisiana field office to Abbeville around 1944 when Hebert replaced Young as resident manager.

With rare exceptions, the meetings of directors were held only once a year at the hunting lodge at Belle Isle after it was constructed and always scheduled during the hunting season in November, a practice continued by Vermilion until 1969. The board approved major decisions at the annual meeting, and, between meetings, the president usually made such decisions in coordination with the resident manager when appropriate.

The surface operations were conducted by the resident manager and his assistants. The primary responsibilities included the trapping, curing and transporting of fur pelts to New York City and providing lodging, meal service, hunting guides and other logistical support and services for the officers and directors and their guests at Belle Isle and on the property during the hunting season. These duties were concentrated in a four-month period from mid-November through the following February. During the balance of the year the employees had limited responsibilities, such as building maintenance, equipment repairs, patrolling against poachers and trespassers, and dredging and conservation projects.

Furs began operations with only two major sources of income—the sale of muskrat and other fur pelts and mineral leases. For the fur trade, Young and Hebert adopted the initials of the Company or "LAFI" as a trade mark stamped on the pelts harvested. The excellent preparation of the pelts by Furs' part-time trappers quickly gained for them a reputation of top quality and usually brought a premium price of "3% to 6% above average for LAFI pelts" in the New York auction market. This premium may have applied only to muskrat pelts, the major income producer. Other pelts marketed under the trade mark stamp were mink, raccoon, and opossum.

In late 1929, Furs, Inc., drafted a five-year contract with New York Auction Company with offices and showrooms on West 26th Street in New York City, for marketing LAFI pelts. Although the record is not clear as to whether a formal contract was ever signed, New York Auction Company in fact served as the exclusive marketing agent for LAFI pelts, at least until late 1939, as confirmed by corporate records and the advertising brochure *Muskrats*, published in 1938: "Since the inception of Louisiana Furs, Inc., its entire annual catch has been marketed through the facilities of the New York Auction Co. . . ."

Hammers not only negotiated the agreement for Furs but he also represented the company in its dealings with New York Auction Company throughout this period. As late as 1938, he advised Furs' Management that he was "still using the New York Auction Co. and feeling well satisfied"; and that the Company through advertising had developed "for LAFI a regular clientele of perhaps 900 buyers in the United States and 200 to 300 each in London and Paris."

But in early 1939, the "chief" of New York Auction died and was replaced by a man about whom Hammers had "reservations" from the outset of his tenure. In a letter dated November 1939, he informed Furs that the New York Auction Company "was going from bad to worse" but indicated also that the new head of the organization was making "a frantic effort to retain the account."

Records are not available to determine whether New York Auction was retained or a substitute marketing agent was contracted. In any event, in the post World War II period, when nutria became the principal pelt in the fur catch, the purchasing agents came to the Abbeville area for the fur auction.

The dramatic fluctuations in the size of the catch and the price of pelts during this eleven-year period are characteristic of the experience of Furs

Corp. and Vermilion to the present time, reinforcing the local belief in a seven-year cycle from peak to nadir in fur trapping. For the season ending February 1928, Furs received probably a record high of $81,464 for its muskrat pelts—far above Vermilion's record—and the landmark first revenues from the property. Although the number of pelts in the harvest that year is not recorded, that number must also have been near a record high.

While the data on price fluctuations are sketchy, the number of muskrat pelts marketed during the years 1930 through 1939 varied from a high of 174,298 in 1931 to a low of 15,707 in 1937. Low harvests were attributed to disease, drought, and other adverse marsh conditions. Prices in 1930 were described as "very low" or forty percent below the prior year; and prices in 1931 were again a drastic sixty-five percent below 1930, reflecting the trough of the depression. And the same trend continued through 1933: "Prices very low . . . . Company's fur revenues very much reduced."

Recovery began in the following year, with "sales taking place at much higher prices (71 cent -77 cent) so that gross income may be higher than with the larger catch of the previous year." Since the 1934 harvest was 20,593 pelts compared to 52,490 in 1933, a decline of over sixty percent, the price in the latter year must have averaged below thirty cents a pelt. In the next two years, the price per muskrat pelt fluctuated from $1.60 to $1.19.[3]

In 1940, an act of nature introduced the South American coypu or nutria to the property and surrounding marshland areas on the Louisiana Gulf Coast. This large aquatic rodent, about three times the size of a muskrat and commercially valuable for its soft brown undercoat, multiplied rapidly in this habitat and in a brief period of time became the principal animal of the trapping trade for Furs, Inc., and successors.

The accidental introduction of the coypu to the habitat was caused by a hurricane of major force which struck the coastal area in 1940, inundating the land a considerable distance from the coast into the interior. E. A. McIlhenny had established a private zoo and aviary on Avery Island, known as Jungle Gardens and Bird Sanctuary, which was, and still is open to the public. Jungle Gardens housed his collection of exotic animals and birds,

---

[3] This pattern has continued throughout Vermilion's history. For example, prior to 1989, the lowest receipts from fur trapping were $2,800 in 1959, the first full year of operations. In 1989, trapping receipts fell below $1,000 or about one-third of the previous record low.

including pens of nutria. These pens reportedly collapsed during the hurricane, releasing the animals to the surrounding natural setting. The long-term result proved to be an indirect but nonetheless valuable bequest of McIlhenny to Furs, Inc.[4]

Two other sources of surface lease income were initiated in 1937 and have continued to the present. At the annual meeting of the board at Belle Isle, Young reported that an initial planting of twenty acres of rice that year "was not very successful, partly due to a high tide against which there was no levee protection." He expressed the opinion that some levee construction could open about 250 acres to rice cultivation in this unidentified area of the property and that "this rice land would be readily rentable." In addition, he estimated that 4,000 to 5,000 acres in the northwest sector of the property could be converted to rice cultivation after some dredging to yield a potential of 20 barrels per acre.

The second revenue producing operation was cattle grazing, a potential source of income considered by the owners of Coast Land. In 1937, Furs, Inc., negotiated a five-year grazing lease with Dr. Martin O. Miller and his brother on the southeastern portion of the property at a price of $1.25 per head of cattle. Dr. Miller and his heirs continued to rent pasture acreage from Furs and successor companies until 1978.

A third revenue-producing operation considered at the same time apparently failed but both Hammers and Young were "quite enthusiastic" about "the possibilities of frog farming." At this annual meeting, the directors "put in Dr. Young's hands full responsibility for development of grazing, cotton and rice prospects; and also authorized him to spend up to $900 or $1,000 for an experimental frog pond."

Commercial frog farming may have been one of the early, rudimentary forms of aquaculture or the man-controlled breeding and cultivation of various species of fish and crustaceans. This experiment was a harbinger of Vermilion's experiment many years later with catfish farming and various attempts to attract the interest of aquaculture enterprises in the potential of the leasehold for this purpose.

* * *

---

[4] According to Pat Adams, the first trapper to catch a nutria on the Furs' property thought he had landed the world's largest muskrat.

A second major source of income for Furs was the sale of mineral leases on the approximate 30,000 acres reserved and excluded from the lease held by McFadden on the rest of the acreage.[5] This income began from the outset of Furs, Inc.'s operations and continued until Furs Corp. was dissolved in 1958. In addition, after oil and gas production began on the reserved acreage, Furs received payments for its 1/8 overriding royalty interest from the production runs until 1952, when it was reorganized and 95 percent of the royalty interest was spun off to the stockholders.

McFadden, the chairman of Southland Royalty Company after 1930, held the same mineral lease on the Coast Land property, which he renewed when Furs, Inc., was organized. In August 1928, he paid $1,000 to Furs, Inc., for a one-year extension. Although he advised the board as late as July that he was "ready to spend $240,000 on seismographic work," his apparent objective was overriding royalty interests from successful working interest owners. He assigned at least a part of his mineral lease to Louisiana Land & Exploration Company for unknown considerations shortly after paying Furs, Inc., for the one-year extension. And he reportedly retained a 1/32 overriding royalty interest on most or all of the acreage not reserved to Furs.[6]

McFadden was a very successful oil company executive with a reputation for identifying land with good mineral prospects. The directors of Furs, Inc., delegated to him a major responsibility for negotiating mineral leases on its reserved acreage. On various occasions, he was able to obtain considerably higher lease or extension payments than the initial offers from oil companies.

A number of oil companies purchased mineral leases on the property over a span of many years, including Louisiana Geophysical Exploration,[7] Louisiana Land & Exploration and Humble. Several smaller companies also purchased leases but let them expire without conducting geophysical exploration or drilling. The outbreak of World War II apparently post-

---

[5] At the time of the Humble acquisition of Furs Corp. in 1958, this reserved mineral acreage was described as "33,000 held under production."

[6] In a letter dated July, 1936, apparently addressed to Sterling Morton, Morgan Hammers expressed the view—without any substantiating evidence—"that McFadden's 1/32 overriding royalty evidently stems from sale of his original lease to Louisiana Geophysical Exploration Co. for undisclosed consideration. . . ." This is a paraphrase of the content of the letter, not the letter itself.

[7] This company went into receivership in 1936 and Louisiana Land & Exploration acquired its mineral lease on the property at a receivership sale in April of that year.

poned for some years the geophysical surveys, exploratory and development drilling and pipeline construction on the property which otherwise would have been undertaken during the period 1941-1946.

The income from mineral leases and bonus payments over many years was critical to the financial stability of both Furs, Inc., and Furs Corp. and probably approached or exceeded the combined total revenues from fur pelts, rice shares, and grazing. For example, the total revenue from four principal leases in 1936 was about $53,000. In the years that followed, Humble reduced its annual payments for lease extensions from $24,000 to $12,000, because of delays in settling disputed claims to title on the boundaries of Furs' property. Two major bonus payments were made during this period, one by Louisiana Land & Exploration for $10,000 and the other by Humble for $25,000, for contracts signed in 1934 and 1935, respectively. These were significant amounts in relation to Furs' annual gross receipts.

The size of the acreage involved was not defined in the corporate records available, with three exceptions. On two of these leases, the per acre payments ranged from $0.25 to $5.00, the former dating back to 1931. For the third lease, Stanolind Oil & Gas Company paid a $750 bonus and granted a 1/8 overriding royalty interest on the ratio of Furs' acreage to the total in the development area. The location was "the Company's small lot at Intracoastal City (2.2 acres)...."

The potential for oil and gas development not only occasionally stimulated "excitement" among the directors but also created a suspicious attitude about any change in the ownership of Furs' stock.

As noted earlier, Young was granted 50 shares in exchange for the cancellation of his unpaid fees for services to Coast Land. Sometime after Mark Hebert replaced Young as resident manager, he was granted and exercised the right to purchase shares in an unknown amount. Pat Adams was also granted the right to buy shares after he became the vice president and secretary-treasurer of Furs, Inc., but initially on the condition that he sell them back to the company in the event he wanted to liquidate. When Adams told the other directors he would purchase shares only if he had complete freedom to do as he pleased with them the day after the purchase, this condition was dropped.

On one occasion in 1937, Young informed the directors of a possible challenge to ownership control of Furs, Inc., because of the land's potential for oil and gas development:

Dr. Young's report mentions inquiry from 'some of the head employees of Humble Oil' as to whether any Louisiana Furs stock might be for sale. Company Directors immediately suspect attempt to get control of Louisiana Furs for oil interests. This excitement coincided with the transfer of 200 shares of stock to the J. Henry Schroeder Banking Corporation. Subsequently, this latter deal turned out to be merely a transfer to the Bank of collateral originally posted by Snyder & Hay.[8]

Taking no chances and "after long negotiations," Morton and McFadden each bought 100 shares at a cost of $100 per share from the Schroeder Banking Corporation in the following year. "This was done solely to prevent the stock from getting into hands which might prove troublesome."

* * *

By the end of 1938, Furs, Inc., had made relatively large capital expenditures for construction of the lodge, employee quarters and other facilities at Belle Isle and for equipment for operations and recreational hunting, including several motor boats, marsh buggies, hunting gear and a second-hand dredge. The construction of the facilities and acquisition of the equipment are believed to have taken place over several years, in contrast to the advertising hyperbole in the Furs' brochure on muskrat pelts: "The property was bought outright, and immediately equipped with splendid company headquarters and complete facilities for the thorough consummation of its aims."

This document also provided an inventory of equipment and a description of the facilities as of 1938:

---

[8] Snyder & Hay had provided legal and other services for Coast Land and held an unpaid invoice of $37,000 against this Company at the time of its bankruptcy. The law firm may have obtained the 200 shares of Furs, Inc., as a compromise settlement of the debt, similar to the settlement with Young.

MUSKRATS

– their origin, habits and habitat.

—◆—

Published in the interests of the Fur Trade
by LOUISIANA FURS, INC.

An important fleet of motor boats, including a fifty-four foot ocean-going cabin cruiser, is maintained by the company. Headquarters buildings are provided with electric lighting plants, refrigeration, automatic water supply and all modern equipment, including agricultural implements, marsh vehicles, etc. There are also fur drying and curing houses with controlled air-conditioning facilities and a series of collecting houses and depots.

One illustration in this brochure is a photograph of the ocean-going vessel with the caption "The Cruiser 'J. M.,' flagship of the fleet of power boats," obviously named in honor of the deceased first president of Furs, Inc., Joy Morton.

With regard to the financial record of Furs, Inc., and the successor Furs Corp., only a brief and generalized analysis can be pieced together from the limited corporate records available. With one exception, the annual financial statements of these two companies are missing and it is not even known whether they were subject to external audit. However, both Furs, Inc., and Furs Corp. apparently had enough paid-in capital from the initial stock offering and operating revenues until the dissolution of the latter in 1958 to more than cover all expenditures without having to borrow funds (excepting possibly occasionally on a short-term basis) or to issue any senior securities. Considering the capital expenditures, this was a major achievement. Moreover, according to the recollections of some living Furs, Inc., stockholders, they received some generous dividend and royalty payments, particularly after 1947, and were rewarded with the royalty spinoff in the reorganization of 1952.

On the other hand, the maintenance of a positive cash flow from operations and mineral leases was at risk in some years; and Furs, Inc., probably had to draw from the capital paid for the stock offering in lean years of income. In the earlier years of Furs, Inc., small sums of money were of considerable significance to the balance sheet and so-called bottom line. After the Bank of Abbeville suspended payments to depositors in early 1932, the company described its account with this institution as "the unusually large deposit of $14,059.49." When Louisiana Land & Exploration Company made a mineral lease payment in 1935 in the amount of $8,448.60, the following notation was entered in one corporate record: "This sum aided greatly to help the Company's cash position. Directors hope for offers from other firms for acreage now being released."

The first divided payment in 1937 was not made to reward the patient stockholders. The following rationale was recorded:

> Chiefly to avoid the undistributed surplus tax an initial dividend of $1.00 per share was paid . . . altho-(*sic*) the Company at that time had an earned deficit and there was some thought the dividend might be illegal under Delaware law unless accompanied by a statement specifically stating that it was being paid from current earnings or capital surplus.[9]

This comment suggests that Furs, Inc., had in fact drawn from the paid-in capital from time to time, if the confusing accounting term "earned deficit" is interpreted as a net loss from operations from 1927 until 1937.

Finally, another general conclusion can be drawn from the data available about the financial record of Furs, Inc., and Furs Corp. which was to characterize Vermilion's surface lease operations for more than twenty years after its organization in 1958. Without the income from mineral leases and later from oil royalties, Furs, Inc., and Furs Corp. probably would have registered deficits of varying magnitudes for most of the years if dependent on the one source of revenue or the expanded three sources after 1937.

Trapping was the only source of significant revenue and it fluctuated dramatically, depending on the size of the harvest and the market price, as indicated earlier. At the close of this precursor era, the combined income from rice shares and grazing was still less than $10,000. The statement of income and expenditures for the fiscal year ending October 31, 1956, produced a loss from surface operations, excluding oil and gas income, of $24,600 before estimated property taxes of $13,600 had been paid.

The balance sheet for the fiscal year 1957 reflects the financial status of Furs Corp. a few months before its liquidation and dissolution. The only three major assets with their estimated value were: Land, $573,000; Buildings & Structures, $6,900; and Furniture, Boats and Equipment, $36,400, the last item being the "tangible moveables" later sold to Vermilion for $25,000 at market rather than book value.

There were only two entries under liabilities and net worth: Liabilities and tax reserves, $258,600; and Earned surplus, $596,300 or $38.80 per share on the 15,366 shares outstanding. Adjusted in reverse for the 5,122

---

[9] Over a ten-year period, this dividend equates to a 0.1% annual yield on a $100 stock.

shares of $100 par value and cost which Furs, Inc., had outstanding in 1952, the per share equivalent would be $116.42.[10]

* * *

The last major event of this precursor era was a corporate reorganization of Furs, Inc., in late 1952. At the first step, the company distributed 95 percent of its 1/8 overriding royalty interest to its stockholders pro rata to the size of their holdings. The royalty payments thereafter were made direct to the owners of the units by the producing oil companies.

Furs Corp. was then organized and incorporated under the laws of Delaware in November 1952. It retained the five percent overriding royalty interest not distributed to the stockholders of Furs, Inc. As the final step in the reorganization, Furs Corp. issued 15,366 shares of its stock in exchange for the 5,122 shares outstanding of Furs, Inc., or a three-for-one ratio. Furs, Inc., distributed the stock to its former stockholders as the final action before its dissolution.

The purpose of the reorganization was to avoid dual corporate and individual taxation on the royalty income when it was distributed to stockholders. For some reasons or reasons, McFadden strongly opposed the proposal when it was discussed at the annual meeting of Directors in November 1952. Possibly feeling that decisions and initiatives related to mineral leases and royalties were his exclusive domain, he became intemperate, and abrasive during the discussion of this item. Nevertheless, the board approved it and the other aspects of the reorganization.[11]

* * *

Throughout the three decades which comprised the era of Furs, Inc., and Furs Corp., there was an unusual continuity of management and com-

---

[10] These data were used during the negotiations with Humble leading to its acquisition of Furs Corp. In 1958. The 1956 statement of income and expenditures was used because severe hurricane damage in fiscal 1957 had disrupted the surface operations to the extent they were not representative. It should be noted that there is no provision under liabilities in the 1957 balance sheet for the value of the 15,366 shares outstanding.

[11] According to a director present at this session, Sterling Morton had a strong reaction to McFadden's comportment and left the meeting room. He apparently suffered a mild heart attack from this confrontation.

position of the boards of directors, with the only known changes resulting from the deaths of the incumbents. There were two presidents (Joy and Sterling Morton); three vice presidents (McFadden, Adams and Dave Wallace); three secretaries (Hammers, Adams and McBride, sometime after 1952); one known treasurer (Adams); and two resident managers (Young and Hebert). Although only Scott Probasco served as a director for the entire period, several others also had a long tenure in this capacity, including Adams, Morton, McFadden (d. 1956), Dave Wallace and Dick Baldwin.

Chapter IV

THE TRANSITION FROM FURS CORP. TO VERMILION - BAYOU

As early as 1955 (and possibly earlier), the board of directors of Furs Corp. informally considered the possibility of establishing a tax-exempt, not-for-profit hunting club for recreational purposes as a distinct corporate entity. The club, as then envisioned, would also control the surface operations under a long-term lease to be granted by Furs Corp., which would retain title to the land, the mineral rights, and the five percent of a 1/8th overriding royalty interest retained in the reorganization and dissolution of Furs, Inc. in 1952. The three lease operations continued to be trapping, grazing, and farming. These discussions apparently arose from the growing disparity between stockholders who used the hunting facilities (primarily directors, their family members and guests) and those who did not hunt or who could not enjoy the facilities for various reasons. The latter was probably a substantial majority by 1957.

At the annual meeting of November 1956, the board formally authorized Lloyd McBride, secretary and general legal counsel, and his law firm to investigate the legal, tax and feasibility aspects of organizing such a club. This proposal, which ultimately was revised, was an interesting reversion to the origins of Furs, Inc., with the Gulf Coast Club and later Coast Land, the former being a recreational organization and the latter a for-profit land management company with a provision for a hunting club.

In reviewing Coast Land's acquisition of the property and financial problems, the law firm of Snyder & Hay in Chicago recommended that a hunting club be organized separate from Coast Land "such as is contemplated by the charter of the Louisiana Gulf Coast Club," in order to avoid the ten percent ad valorem "initiation fee" on the $2,000 per share price of the stock certificates:

> As a matter of fact, the Internal Revenue department has already leveed such assessments on the theory that the Louisiana Coast Land Company has been and is operating as a club, but it

is our opinion, if the records which we have in our possession are complete . . . that this assessment can be defeated.[1]

McBride, Baker et al. had a similar problem in establishing a hunting club with control over for-profit, revenue-producing operations, such as grazing, trapping, and farming, unrelated to recreational sports activities. By 1958, the ad valorem tax on membership certificates in certain types of recreational clubs had risen to 20 percent.

While the investigation into the club reorganization was in the early stage, Humble Oil initiated negotiations in January 1957 to acquire the assets of Furs Corp. and the royalty interests distributed to Furs, Inc., stockholders in the 1952 reorganization and dissolution of Furs, Inc., on the approximate 33,000 acres then under production. During negotiations through most of 1957, the two parties established conditions precedent to consummation of an agreement. Humble Oil reserved the right to withdraw its offers unless two-thirds of Furs Corp. stockholders approved the terms and also unless 85 percent or more of the royalty units outstanding were tendered. Advising Humble at the outset of its plan for reorganizing into a for-profit corporation to control certain surface operations and a not-for-profit hunting club, Furs Corp. conditioned its acceptance on Humble's approval of the terms of a long-term surface lease and hunting sublease applicable to the entire 125,000 acres.

After receipt of the terms of Humble's offers for the stock and separately owned royalty units in late 1957, Vermilion was organized and incorporated under the laws of Delaware in March 1958. At the same time, Furs Corp. granted Vermilion a 99-year surface lease "for the sole purpose of hunting migratory water fowl, trapping, and otherwise capturing fur bearing animals and alligators, and for farming and pasturing." (Humble, the succeeding lessor, and Vermilion negotiated an amendment to this lease the following February which expanded Vermilion's surface operations to include the hunting of game and fishing.) The consideration to be paid by the lessee was an annual rental of $5,000.00 or a contingent rental of 10 percent of gross income from lease operations, whichever was larger.

Vermilion also signed a contract with Furs Corp. to buy all "tangible moveables" from the latter for $25,000, or what was considered a far market price after depreciation, payable without interest not later than December

---

[1] In April 1926, the U. S. Treasury Department ruled in favor of Coast Land; that is, it was not operated as a club to that time and therefore not subject to the ad valorem tax.

31, 1958. The tangible moveables included boats, marsh buggies, maintenance and power equipment and furnishings at the lodging quarters at Belle Isle.

The next step was the organization of Bayou Corp. under the laws of Illinois as a not-for-profit hunting club, which gained tax-exempt status shortly after completing its first year of operation, as required under the federal revenue code. Vermilion granted Bayou a hunting and fishing sublease on the entire acreage with a term of 98 years, or coinciding closely to the 99 years the Vermilion lease was to run. Vermilion reserved the right to sell short-term hunting subleases on the perimeter of the property, outside and a certain distance from the approximate 44,000 interior acreage reserved exclusively by Bayou members, members of their families and other guests—the Bayou Reserved Area. The sale of leases on the Vermilion reserved perimeter became a fourth source of revenue from the outset of Vermilion operations and has ranked by far the largest for many years.

Among the considerations for the Bayou sublease, Bayou was obligated to pay a fixed per acre annual rental on the entire approximate 125,000 acres. This amount was reduced by a formula based on Bayou's per acre rental multiplied times the number of acres Vermilion rented in the perimeter area outside Bayou's Reserve. The resulting figure was in turn multiplied by a fraction equal to the length of the hunting season allowed as a percentage of the full 365-day year (usually 70/365). In addition, Bayou had a contingent rental obligation in those years in which Vermilion incurred an operating deficit after combining all sources of revenue. This contingent rental was equal to the deficit, after various allowable deductions specified in the terms of the contract.

Vermilion was obligated to provide Bayou members and guests with various hunting facilities, services, and equipment and service personnel during the hunting seasons and also to maintain the equipment and facilities during the seasons and off-season periods on a compensable or reimbursement of cost basis.

At that time, McBride and Adams had solid reasons to believe that the prospects for Vermilion to break-even or achieve modest profitability would be bleak for some years. They could not foresee the development of the new sources of lease operations or the revenues to be generated by non-lease surface operations, such as pipeline and other easements and commercial land-lease rentals, later to be shared equally between Humble/Exxon and Vermilion. The guideline was the heavy loss Furs Corp. would have incurred in fiscal 1956 from the surface operations alone.

The language of the hunting and fishing sublease clearly reflects the concern of the incorporators and other principals about Vermilion's financial future:

> ... Sublessor shall diligently seek to generate gross income and to control costs so as to avoid or minimize net deficits and so as to create and add to earned surplus.

The Bayou board of directors approved the hunting and fishing sublease in August 1958 and it became effective in November of that year. During the organizational period, Furs Corp. advised Humble that ten membership certificates would be reserved by Bayou for Humble executives and these were promptly purchased after they were tendered. Carl E. Reistle, Jr., chairman of Humble, was elected as one of the charter board members of Bayou. Oral Luper and Nelson Jones, both Bayou members and retired Exxon executives, have served on the Vermilion board since December 1983 and 1985, respectively.

The Humble tender offers for Furs Corp. stock and the royalty units were received in late 1957, and all conditions of the two parties were satisfied by the end of March 1958, except the minimum tender of royalty units imposed by Humble. The terms of the offers, scheduled to expire on July 1, 1958, were as follows: Humble offered 14 shares of its stock for each of the 15,366 of Furs outstanding or a total of 215,124 of the former worth about $11,700,000.[2] In a separate tender made through Furs Corp., Humble offered $976.18 per royalty unit for the 5,122 units outstanding for a total value of $5,000,000. Humble is believed to have acquired all of the Furs stock outstanding and probably more than 95 percent of the royalty units.

As a part of the acquisition, Humble assumed all of the assets and liabilities of Furs Corp. when it was placed in dissolution after distributing the Humble shares to its former stockholders. Apart from the 5 percent of one-eighth overriding royalty interest, the major items and the value on the books at the time were as follows: land ($573,000); buildings and structures ($6,900); the payment due for furniture, boats, vehicles, and

---

[2] Closing prices of Humble stock then traded on the American Stock Exchange on March 3, 27 and 31 were $50, $53.30 and $54.50, respectively. In 1959, Jersey Standard acquired the 30 percent of Humble it did not own in a tender of five shares of the former for four shares of the latter.

equipment ($25,000); liabilities and tax reserves ($258,600); and the earned surplus ($596,300) or $38.80 per share on the 15,366 shares outstanding.

McBride, Baker et al., which was assigned the duty of making arrangements for activating both Vermilion and Bayou, submitted its recommendations on the former in March to a small group of officers and stockholders of Furs Corp., including Morton and Adams. A special stockholders meeting was called in June to approve the activating proposals presented in their final form.

The initial stock offering was in units of 170 shares each at a price of $10.00 per share, submitted to eligible purchasers on June 23 with an expiration date of July 21. Of a total of 74 former eligible owners of Furs, 58 exercised their rights and 16 did not.

At a board meeting in August, McBride was authorized to make a second offering of 2,720 undersubscribed shares to the new stockholders of Vermilion and issue the certificates on a pro-rata basis in the event the offer was oversubscribed. The maximum number of shares purchased by any one stockholder in the second offering was 96 and the paid-in capital from both offers was $125,570 at the close of the first full year of operations, ending August 31, 1959, or 12,557 shares outstanding.[3] 3

To complete the activation of Vermilion, a special meeting of stockholders was convened on August 14, 1958 in Chicago for election of directors. The first board of directors was composed of Daniel Peterkin, Jr., Richard Baldwin, David A. Wallace, Frank A. Knapp, Clayton J. Adams, Scott L. Probasco and George A. Lyon, Jr.

At the Board meeting which followed, the following officers were elected: Richard Baldwin, president; Dan Peterkin, Jr., vice president; J. Mark Hebert, vice president and general manager; Lloyd McBride, secretary and general legal counsel; and E. J. Kibbe, assistant secretary.

John Donohue, of the accounting firm of Donohue and Poché in Abbeville, was later chosen treasurer and still serves in this capacity at the present time. Donohue was later chosen vice president and general manager in 1972 and to the position of president and chief executive officer in December 1988. In December 1976 he was elected a director and has also served as secretary during the period 1984-1988.

This protracted transition period began in late 1956 with the Furs Corp. directive to McBride to investigate the feasibility of reorganizing Furs to grant the surface operations on the land and the tangible moveables

---

[3] As of December, 1989, the shares outstanding of Vermilion stock have varied by less than 1,125 shares.

to a hunting club under a long-term lease and ended with the liquidation and dissolution of Furs Corp. and the activation of Vermilion and Bayou. One conclusion is obvious: The primary and overriding objective was to preserve the superb recreational hunting on a leasehold which reportedly was a habitat for a substantial percentage of the migratory duck and goose population on the Louisiana Gulf Coast.

Vermilion was organized as a risky investment but a necessary mechanism to preserve the hunting rights, services, and facilities. Therefore, without the hunting habitat, Furs Corp. would probably have had no successor organization after its dissolution. Ironically, in the tradition of Furs, Inc., and Furs Corp., Vermilion proved in time to be an excellent investment.

CHAPTER V

CONSERVATION OF THE LEASEHOLD

Ecological and environmental conservation of the leasehold has been a heavy and increasing responsibility confronting management almost from the outset of Vermilion's operations. Some adverse effects were caused by the private canals dredged prior to 1958, but the employees of Furs, Inc., and Furs Corp. controlled them with bank containment levees and water structures. Except in times of exposure to hurricanes, tropical storms and other severe weather, the exchange of water between the western sector of Vermilion Bay and the tributaries draining into the bay from the leasehold was gradual and without extreme turbidity or turbulence.

The problems were greatly exacerbated in the early 1960s when the U. S. Corps of Engineers began construction of the Freshwater Bayou Canal and increased after this huge channel was opened to public marine traffic in 1968. Pronounced changes occurred in many sectors of the leasehold from resulting salt water intrusion, increased water salinity in the man-made and natural tributaries, canal bank and levee erosion and the increased velocity of water exchange from tidal action in Vermilion Bay between the leasehold and the bay. The ecological and environmental damage stretched far beyond the areas adjacent to the public Freshwater Bayou Canal banks.

As noted in Chapter One, Vermilion made a concerted effort in its early years to oppose the choice of the Freshwater Bayou route by the Corps of Engineers for access from the Intracoastal Canal to the Gulf of Mexico in this sector of the Louisiana coast. It recommended the Vermilion Bay route through Southwest Pass between the mainland and Marsh Island. The prophetic arguments set forth in support of the latter route were based on cost-benefit ratios, maintenance, engineering and geological factors. But the primary emphasis was placed on the potential for extreme adverse impacts on the wildlife habitat and the wildlife, if the Freshwater Bayou route were selected in contrast to minimal harm from the use of Vermilion Bay - Southwest Pass.

The document presenting the comparative analysis of the two routes and the conclusions and recommendations in favor of the Freshwater Bayou route of the Board of Engineers for Rivers and Harbors, Corps of Engineers was entitled *Survey of Fresh Water Bayou and Vicinity, Louisiana* (hereinafter referred to as *Corps Survey*), dated September 15, 1958. The recommendation was officially announced in January 1959; and Vermilion was notified in May by the New Orleans District Engineer that those in opposition to the recommended route should submit their views on or before June 12. The Board of Engineers for Rivers and Harbors subsequently granted Vermilion's request for an extension of the deadline until August 11, 1959.

Vermilion directors were aware that a large public canal was being considered to link the Intracoastal Waterway with the Gulf of Mexico in the general area of the location of the Vermilion leasehold. But they did not learn until December 1958

> . . . and then only by rumor rather than by official notice that a recommendation had been made or was about to be made by the United States Army Engineer District, New Orleans, Corps of Engineers, in favor of the Fresh Water Bayou route for the canal in question.

The Vermilion effort to block the selection of this route is reviewed here as a landmark in the conservation programs of the Company which has always given this objective considerable priority in a rational way, taking into consideration the economic and other interests of the community of Vermilion Parish and surrounding parishes.

The Vermilion board of directors immediately recognized the probability of potential serious damage to the wildlife, wildlife habitat, trapping and other operations on the leasehold from construction of a large public canal through the property. There were also potential problems of a secondary nature, such as increased poaching and trespassing in the lateral private canals and the increased costs of patrolling and surveillance for which Vermilion was responsible to Humble, its lessor.

The board authorized a preliminary investigation to identify the best means to oppose the Corps' recommended route and to support the alternate route under consideration through the Bay and the Southwest Pass. The directors were aware that the implementation of an effective plan would probably be costly for a small corporation like Vermilion, recently organized with a paid-in capital from the two stock offerings of $125,557 and a long-term outlook for deficits in its lease operations.

By early January 1959, the plan of opposition had been devised. The board directed McBride to carry out the measures, acting jointly with

Edmund McIlhenny, a partner in the law firm of Chaffee McCall, Phillips et al. in New Orleans, in both Louisiana and Washington, D. C., to enlist support in opposition to the recommended canal route from interested government agencies and environmental groups. This was McIlhenny's first assignment as Vermilion's Louisiana legal counsel.

Pursuant to another board authorization, McIlhenny assembled a group of expert specialists in various fields to gather additional factual data omitted from the *Corps Survey*; to correct any errors of fact or interpretation uncovered in that document; and to prepare reports on their independent studies. The final composite document, printed in Chicago, was entitled *Survey and Report of Vermilion Corporation in Opposition to Project*, dated August 10, 1959 (hereinafter referred to as *Vermilion Survey*).

There were four topical reports in the composite dealing with "Economics," "Engineering," "Geology," and "Wildlife," as related to the two canal routes under consideration. The composite totaled about 104 pages, excluding a number of exhibits, annexes, and maps. Eight experts in different fields made contributions.[1] McIlhenny and McBride prepared the six-page "Introduction," which provided detail on the background of the study and also summarized the "Salient Features of This Survey and Report."

Each specialist reached the conclusion that cost-benefit ratios in all areas—engineering, construction and maintenance—clearly favored the Vermilion Bay-Southwest Pass route. The geological study suggested that any savings to the offshore oil industry would at best be nominal from construction of a canal through the Vermilion leasehold compared to the Southwest Pass route.

In limiting damage to wildlife, its habitat and other commercial activities on the Vermilion leasehold, the evidence presented was overwhelmingly in favor of the alternate route. In fact, the *Corps Survey*

---

[1] The experts, the positions they held at that time and the titles which they prepared or to which they made contributions are as follows: Stephen L. McDonald, Ph. D., Chairman, Department of Finance, Louisiana State University (LSU) (Economics), with contributions from John P. Donohue, Independent Public Accountant and Treasurer of Vermilion; Harry E. Bovay, Jr., Consulting Engineer, Baton Rouge and Houston (Engineering); Richard J. Russell, Dean, Graduate School, LSU (Geology); Richard K. Yancey, Chief, Refuge Division, Louisiana Wildlife and Fisheries Commission; Leslie L. Glasgow, Ph. D., Professor of Game Management, School of Forestry, LSU; Ted O'Neil, Chief, Furs Division, Louisiana Wildlife and Fisheries Commission; and J. Mark Hebert, Vice President and General Manager, Vermilion (Wildlife).

did not include any cost factor in its cost-benefit ratio estimates for such potential damages.

The report on "Wildlife" in the *Vermilion Survey* quotes the *Corp Survey* as merely recognizing potential damages from two causes associated with the canal:

> 'Excessive drainage of the marsh and salt water intrusion from Gulf are two major factors which might be expected to affect adversely the general area if the proposed channel connecting the Gulf were uncontrolled.'

The *Corps Survey* then asserted that a lock constructed near the terminus of the Fresh Water Bayou Canal at the gulf would correct and control these problems.

The "Wildlife" report in the *Vermilion Survey* strongly challenged this conclusion. It emphasized that the major ecological problem would not be at the gulf lock but alternately from increased velocity of salt water intrusion and marsh drainage from tidal action in the northwestern section of Vermilion Bay:

> Since the proposed canal will be left wide open and connected directly to Vermilion Bay at its north end, water levels and conditions will vary directly with those in the northwestern section of the Bay. No provisions are included in the work plan to prevent interchange of water from the Bay into the navigational channel and its adjacent marshes. Therefore, the tributary area which comprises nearly 105,000 acres will alternately drain or flood, depending on water levels in Vermilion bay.

The "Wildlife" report then described the migratory wildfowl populations as of that era at the peak of the wintering season on the leasehold. Based on data gathered by the Louisiana Wildlife and Fisheries Commission, the average over the previous five years (1954-1958) was up to 1,000,000 ducks; 25,000 geese; and 40,000 coots or "up to 40% of the overall wintering waterfowl population of Louisiana."

The authors concluded that the most nutritious feeding areas, totaling over 51,000 estimated acres of wild millet, widgeon grass and bull tongue vegetation would all be exposed to serious salt water intrusion and converted into relatively useless wire grass marshes, which could support

Conservation of the Leasehold

only about one duck per acre. Not only would the migratory wildfowl population decline drastically by 75 percent for ducks and 80 percent for coots, but many of the bird species native to the area would be affected similarly. The estimated decline in the population of fur-bearing animals was 50 percent for nutria, muskrat, mink, raccoon, and otter.

The specialists contributing to the "Wildlife" section estimated that damages to the leasehold habitat from the Freshwater Bayou route would result in the course of a few years in annual economic loss of about $495,000. Of this amount, $378,000 would be attributable to the sharply declining population of wildfowl and deer and the balance of $117,000 to a fifty percent decline per acre of furbearing animals and losses from the harvest of alligators and bullfrogs.[2]

In summation these specialists made the following dire prognostication which they indicated would occur within three years or less, of course not taking into account future mitigative actions:

> Approximately 104,000 acres of marshes east and west of the Freshwater Bayou route will be adversely affected from increased drainage and salt water intrusion from Vermilion Bay. Wildlife losses will occur as a result of marsh habitat deterioration. Desirable food plants such as wild millet and widgeon grass will be largely replaced by salt marsh plants such as salt grass and wire grass.

The *Vermilion Survey* was filed with the Corps of Engineers in Washington, D. C., in time to meet the extended deadline for filing opposition views to the Freshwater Bayou route. Then, after the approval was given by the chief engineer for this route, the proposed project had to be submitted to the U. S. Departments of Agriculture and Interior, the Bureau of the Budget, and the governor of the state of Louisiana with a 90-day limit on responses. After this period had lapsed, any interested party could appeal the decision to the secretary of the army.

By April 1960, McBride and McIlhenny believed they had enlisted ". . . the solid support of our opposition to the Freshwater Bayou canal route in all the federal agencies and in the Department of Conservation of the State

---

[2] The above figures have been rounded to the nearest $1,000. Prices for fur pelts used in this study were adjusted to the average over a 17-year period, based on the harvest cycle of the Wildlife and Fisheries Commission of 12 to 20 years from peak to trough and return to peak.

of Louisiana."[3] In addition, McIlhenny had obtained the backing of the Wildlife Management Association, an influential environmental lobbying organization in Washington, D. C. At that juncture, the Vermilion Board authorized additional funds for continuation of their opposition efforts.

By mid-June 1961, however, McBride and McIlhenny reluctantly agreed that any further effort to oppose the project, which Congress had then authorized, by trying to block the appropriations bill "would be fruitless and would only result in wasting efforts and money on legal fees and expenses."[4] A final decision had to be made on the *fait accompli*. This choice was acceptance of a nominal or reasonable sum for the right-of-way, which was not covered by federal funding and Vermilion Parish had to provide, and additional funds to build water control structures to limit the damage from water exchanges or undertake expensive legal condemnation proceedings. On the recommendation of McBride and McIlhenny, the Vermilion board chose the former as in the best long-range interests of the corporation and also because there was no assurance of ultimate success with the latter choice.

A final agreement was reached among the parties involved by April 1962. Humble donated its share of the right-of-way payment with the express request to the police jury of Vermilion Parish that Vermilion be made the beneficiary of this action. Vermilion received $20,000 from the parish for the right-of-way but no allowance for spoil right-of-way. The parish also allotted $63,000 to be held in escrow by Humble for construction of fifteen water-control structures to limit the damages from drainage and salt-water intrusion from the public canal, with payments to be made as costs were incurred during construction. At least, at the time of initiation of work on the canal, Vermilion had in place the funds for a water management program to mitigate the adverse effects.

In addition, in the course of time, the Corps of Engineers had become increasingly aware of the environmental and ecological problems caused by the Freshwater Bayou Canal and the relatively dense marine traffic using it since the lock was completed in 1968. It should be noted that the Corps has invested several millions of dollars in recent years in dredging, building and maintaining spoil bank levees to control salt water intrusion

---

[3] Records do not indicate whether the Governor of Louisiana was approached or his reaction.

[4] The fees for the specialists who prepared the composite *Vermilion Survey* and "the heavy printing costs" for that document—the quoted phrase from a McBride letter—comprised the largest single expenditure in the opposition effort.

Conservation of the Leasehold

and contain bank erosion within the canal.

Many of the adverse effects forecast by the *Vermilion Survey* obviously have occurred on the Vermilion leasehold. Today the continuing efforts of management and employees to implement mitigative plans, such as the installation of water-control structures, levee maintenance and construction, and others, have often been frustrated and delayed by the growing number of federal, state and local agencies involved in the review of proposals and granting of permits. Often these agencies have contradictory objectives and thus conflicting bureaucratic turfs to defend and have established detailed paperwork requirements. The multiple permits now precedent to the initiation of conservation work can drag on from a few months into the years, at a great-to-exorbitant cost in money and man hours, particularly for a small company like Vermilion. In the meanwhile, the environmental or ecological problem needing correction can worsen often in proportion to delays in taking mitigative actions.

Since the start of construction and after the completion of the Freshwater Bayou Canal, Vermilion's conservation efforts have concentrated primarily on mitigating the adverse effects on the leasehold caused by this navigation route. Unfortunately, the "Wildlife" report in the *Vermilion Survey* proved more than prescient in its evaluation. The point is well illustrated by extracts from a letter of the director of the Louisiana Wildlife and Fisheries Commission to the district engineer in New Orleans, dated July 14, 1975, about seven years after the Canal was opened to traffic:

> The interior marshlands in Vermilion Parish east of Highway 82 and south of Pecan Island are and have been in a condition of serious deterioration for a number of years. This was brought about by increased tidal action and salt water intrusion by cutting of hundreds of miles of canals and ditches through this area . . . mainly for convenience of access and navigation. Marked changes in the ecology of the area have been the result. Salt scalds south of Pecan Island have opened up thousands of acres of once healthy productive marshes that are now largely shallow, muddy, and generally non-productive open bodies of water subject to tidal exchange. In 1959 there were only 1200 acres of wire grass . . . between Pecan Island and the Louisiana Furs Canal and between Highway 82 and what is now the Freshwater Bayou Canal south of Schooner Bayou. Now there are at least 10,000 acres of wire grass and scalded out marsh in this region. . . . In coastal Louisi-

ana wire grass provides one of the best indicators of undesirable change since it rapidly follows the advance of tidal action and salt water intrusion into new areas. In 1959, there were approximately 30,000 acres of wild millet in the area described above as lying north of Louisiana Furs Canal and west of what is now the Freshwater Bayou Canal . . . . Waterfowl use was approximately eight times higher in this area than it was in the wire grass region south of the Louisiana Furs Canal and east of what is now the Freshwater Bayou Canal. As wire grass has invaded the areas waterfowl use has declined proportionately. Had it not been for the fact that spoil levees were constructed along the west bank of the Freshwater Navigational Channel and the fact that Vermilion Corporation has systematically managed to control exchanges of water from the navigational channel in and out of the marsh to the west deterioration in the ecology of this area would have greatly accelerated beyond current levels.

* * *

Two other major developments on the leasehold in recent years either have in fact caused, or had the potential of causing considerable damage to the ecology, although not approaching the magnitude of the effects of the Freshwater Bayou Canal.

Several years ago, the Rockefeller Refuge dredged a canal from the western part of the Pecan Island area southward along its eastern boundary with the Vermilion leasehold to Rollover Bayou, which has an outlet in the Gulf of Mexico. Spoil levees to prevent salt water intrusion were constructed only on the Refuge's west bank of the canal, leaving the Vermilion bank unprotected. Over a period of years, several thousand acres of Vermilion property were scalded by salt water overflows from the Gulf.

The Louisiana Department of Wildlife and Fisheries, which operates the neighboring Refuge, recognized its responsibility for this conservation problem and by early 1984 had completed construction of a weir, other water-control structures and a containment levee on the Vermilion canal bank in order to restore the acreage adversely affected, to the extent possible, to its former condition. The cost of work and installations was over $1,000,000 or above Vermilion's record high year for gross revenues from all sources, illustrating the burdensome costs of correcting man-made damages to areas with delicate ecological balance, such as marshes and wetlands.

The second development was a proposed by-pass channel to be dredged on the eastern bank of Freshwater Bayou Canal around the lock near the Gulf of Mexico. Sohio Company sought a right-of-way for this project in order to permit the transit to the gulf of ocean-going barges with a draft and beam too large to navigate the lock. The barges were to transport heavy modular oil equipment scheduled for construction at facilities in New Iberia. Because of the number of jobs involved and cost economics relative to construction facilities in other locations, there was considerable pressure from local interested groups, the office of the governor of Louisiana and other quarters to win the Sohio contract for New Iberia.

The Vermilion board of directors confronted a thorny dilemma when it met in December 1985 under a short deadline to make its decision on the grant of the right-of-way, caught between the political and economic pressures and the potential ecological problems from the dredging of such a wide elliptical channel. The central issue for Vermilion was totally unrelated to increasing any payment for the grant, which was shared equally with Exxon; but rather to obtain official and other "insurance policies" to correct and prevent, if possible, any future damage to the leasehold. None could accurately forecast this potential damage at that time.

Ultimately, the right-of-way was jointly approved by Vermilion and Exxon Company, U. S. A., which years earlier had become the succeeding lessor to Humble Oil. Sohio contributed a substantial sum to be held in escrow by Exxon for water control structures to mitigate any environmental damages. In addition, Louisiana state agencies, with authority and responsibility, provided guarantees of maintenance of the two closures to the channel after the barges had entered the gulf, maintenance of the banks against erosion and other corrective measures, if required. No serious ecological problems have arisen thus far from dredging the by-pass channel around the lock.

* * *

In 1983, Vermilion launched a new and on-going conservation-management program designed to reduce the continuing increase in the time periods for obtaining multiple approvals and permits from federal, state and local authorities involved for environmental mitigation work and conservation projects. The large area of the leasehold is now in process of being subdivided into land conservation and restoration units with delineated boundaries. With the assistance and guidance of the Soil Conservation Service, U. S. Department of Agriculture, Vermilion employees are defining the units, gathering technical and other data in field surveys and preparing the documentation required by government agencies for assessment prior to the grant of permits for conservation work. With most or all of the required data on file about each land unit with the agencies involved in the approval process, it is believed they will be able to make decisions about conservation projects much more rapidly than has been the case in the past.

William P. Edwards, III, the assistant general manager of Vermilion since July 1980, is a principal contributor to the conservation management program. A native of Abbeville, he has had considerable experience in land an wildlife management. Before joining Vermilion, he served as a volunteer ranger in the conservation training program at Canyonlands National Park, Utah; spent six months in Kenya studying the wildlife, ecology and terrain of that country; and spent a brief period in Central America, participating in specialized ecological studies.

CHAPTER VI

THE EXPANSION AND EVOLUTION OF INCOME-PRODUCING LEASE AND NON-LEASE OPERATIONS

After the Humble acquisition of the assets and liabilities of Furs Corp., the primary purpose of the newly organized Bayou Corporation was to preserve the recreational hunting of migratory wildfowl on the property and retain access to the hunting facilities and services. The membership of the hunting club was essentially the same as the directors, officers, their family members and other guests of Furs Corp. who had enjoyed this sports activity over many years, with the exception of course of the new members sponsored by Humble who subscribed to the memberships set aside for them.

The new Vermilion Corporation had only three established lease operations inherited from Furs, which had a deficit of more than $27,000 on these operations as late as 1956. Vermilion obviously appeared to be highly speculative from an investment standpoint and its viability in question without Bayou's coverage of deficits under terms of the hunting and fishing sublease. Moreover, Vermilion had paid to Humble $25,000 for the tangible moveables at Belle Isle from its $125,500 of working capital received from the two stock offerings.

Vermilion's principal *raison d'être* was to provide hunting facilities, equipment and services and full- and part-time employees for members of Bayou during the hunting season and strive to achieve its "for-profit" organizational status. It was obligated to minimize costs and strive to build an earned surplus which would eliminate in time Bayou's exposure to the contingent rental or coverage of deficits. In other words, as noted earlier, without the valuable hunting conditions on the leasehold and facilities in place at Belle Isle, Vermilion would probably not have been organized.

Ironically, over the years, the corporation had the opportunity to expand the lease operations considerably compared to its predecessors—hunting permits outside Bayou's Reserved Area, alligator, shrimping, fishing and crayfish shares and most recently the sale of alligator eggs to commercial alligator farm operators. It was also the recipient in 1964 and afterwards of substantial revenues shared equally with Humble (and the successor Exxon

Company) of third-party commercial land subleases, pipeline and other easements, canal-use permits and payments for rights-of-way. None of these sources was comprehended in the surface lease which defined Vermilion's exclusive surface operations.

In addition, in the years since 1984, Vermilion has received substantial and unexpected payments for surface damages from seismic operations conducted for third parties on the property. Most of the commercial land sub-leases and the non-recurring sources of income are directly or indirectly attributable to onshore and offshore activities and requirements of the oil and gas industry since 1958. Thus, the history of Furs, Inc., and Furs Corp. did in fact repeat itself in large degree in the Vermilion financial experience. Vermilion shares were eventually to be converted into a valuable investment by conventional criteria from developments closely related to the energy industry.

By the end of its first full year of operations on August 31, 1959, Vermilion had established a major new source of lease income from the sale of hunting permits.[1] This source was to become the uncontested, highest ranking producer of gross receipts from lease operations after 1977, exceeding in that year and most subsequent years—usually by a substantial margin—the total of shared receipts from recurring and non-recurring sources specified in the Joint Land Management Agreement, to be described later in this chapter.

The sale of these permits was a consideration retained by Vermilion under the terms of the hunting and fishing sublease granted to Bayou, provided they did not impinge on Bayou's interior Reserved Area of about 44,000 acres and were at least two miles from the perimeter of this reserve. In only four years from 1959 to the present did any other lease operation, as defined in the surface lease originally granted by Furs Corp. to Vermilion and inherited by Humble, exceed the receipts from hunting permits. In 1966, 1969, 1974, and 1977, trapping shares ranked first, but only by a small margin.

Over a period of about fourteen years, income from hunting permits remained relatively stable, ranging from $24,000 to $37,000 annually. After 1972, the per acre price has been increased gradually to reflect the rates for similar acreage in this sector of the Louisiana Gulf Coast; and in recent years have averaged about $300,000 annually. The importance of these

---

[1] It seems inexplicable that the directors and management of Furs, Inc., and Furs Corp. did not exploit this valuable source of revenue.

receipts to Vermilion's financial status and health cannot be exaggerated, an attribute which applied not only during the early years but down to the present.

If this source of reliable revenue had not been available at the beginning of operations, both Vermilion and Bayou would probably have had a difficult time struggling with financial survival. For example, during the first seven years of operation—1959 through 1965—hunting lease rentals produced about $218,000 of the total gross revenues of $452,000 from all sources (including non-lease and interest income) or 48 percent of this total. The receipts from hunting permits covered 56 percent of total operating expenditures of over $387,400 during this period.[2] If the revenue from hunting permits were deleted, the annual deficit for these seven years would have averaged over $22,000.

Trapping shares in the first seven years were gradually recovering from the low of the trapping cycle at less than $3,000 in 1959 to more than $13,000 in 1965. Thereafter until 1982, this source of income consistently made substantial contributions to Vermilion's gross receipts, recording an all-time high of over $74,000 in 1977. Subsequently, with the exception of 1985 and 1987, trapping shares have been declining to a new all-time low of less than $1,000 in 1989. Over the eight-year period since 1982, the average return from trapping had been less than $14,000 annually.

In recent years, adverse climatic conditions have reduced the size of the nutria and muskrat harvest; and market prices for these fur pelts have generally been declining. In addition, the fur industry has faced strong opposition and adverse publicity from environmental and animal rights groups which have been accompanied by a declining consumer demand for fur products in the United States and Western Europe. As a result, the prospects for the recovery of trapping income to anything approaching the average of the past thirty-one years, or $25,900, appear problematical into the foreseeable future.

With regard to the other two lease operations established by Furs, Inc., in 1937, grazing fees have generally registered a gradual but steady increase over three decades, from a beginning of just over $4,000 in 1959 to a high of $19,500 in 1983, averaging about $18,000 over the last six-year period of 1984-1989, inclusive. Much of the increase is attributable to upward adjustments of the per head, per acre fee; but it also reflects the larger

---

[2] Bayou annual payments for compensable services are deleted from both gross income and expenditures.

size of the cattle herds grazing on the leasehold. Over the past decade, grazing fees have been one of the most stable of Vermilion's leasehold operations, with the lowest percentage fluctuations from high to low in this period.

In contrast, rice shares have seldom provided more than a modest income, with the exception of four years when the receipts ranged from $12,000 to a record high of over $25,000 in 1975. For the balance of 27 years, the income ranged from a low of $800 to a high of $11,400. The average for the entire 31-year period has been less than $8,300 or approximately double the income which Furs Corp. was receiving from rice shares at the time of its dissolution in 1958.

A second new source of lease operating income from fishing and crayfish harvests was initiated in 1972 and has produced modest annual yields, ranging from a low of about $700 in 1977 to a high of over $9,000 in 1982. The average over the 18-year period has been about $3,900. The crayfish are harvested primarily from shallow ponds with containment embankments by tenants on the property and the balance is taken from the rice fields.

The year 1974 was a landmark for establishing another major new source of lease operating income—shares obtained from the sale of alligator hides—which in 1982 replaced trapping shares in the number two ranking. The Louisiana Department of Wildlife and Fisheries permitted a controlled, one-month season for capturing alligators in 1974 after this animal was removed from the endangered species list. The hunters are required to register with the department and purchase a hunting license and also must obtain special tags for the hides which the department allocates to the participating property owners. At the outset, the harvest was limited to nine coastal parishes but was expanded state-wide in 1981.

The Department of Wildlife and Fisheries now determines the allowable number of animals in the annual harvest based upon its surveys of the total alligator population, which is the basis of the quota allotment to specific landowners. Income from the harvest is affected by a number of factors, such as the size of the tag quota; average length of the animals captured; and the market price per foot of hide. The season has been permitted in every year since 1974, expecting two suspensions in 1975 and 1979.

Vermilion's income from alligator shares has fluctuated dramatically from a low of $12,600 in 1976 to a record high of $108,600 in 1989, averaging a substantial of $37,000 annually for the fourteen seasons permitted since 1974. This source is now a major contributor to gross revenues.

Closely related is the sale of alligator eggs for breed stock to commercial alligator farm operators. Since 1987, the Department of Wildlife and Fisheries has been delegated authority to issue licenses to qualifying operators and regulate their operations, including control over the number of eggs allowed to be removed from a landholding during any given nesting season. In a delicate series of operations, the eggs are removed from the nests on the leasehold, placed in special racks in the same position as on the nest and transported to farm facilities for incubation.

In 1988 and 1989, the only two years of experience with these sales, Vermilion has received $60,000 and $76,000, respectively, including a bonus of $1.00 for each surviving hatchling from G. C. Alligator Farm, the largest operator involved with Vermilion. This enterprise is located at Grand Chenier, near the gulf coast and about 30 miles west of the settlement of Pecan Island. G. C. Alligator Farm has a long-term supply contract with a Parisian firm which cures the hides for manufacturing into finished products.

The Department of Wildlife and Fisheries requires the return of 17 percent of the surviving hatchlings to the original habitat after they reach a certain length which favors their survival, particularly against the cannibalism of mature alligators. The replacement step is the final one in the cycle. When eggs are left in the natural habitat, only an estimated five percent hatch and survive to maturity because of the many bird and animal predators on the leasehold.

Another new source of revenue was opened by the Department of Wildlife and Fisheries in 1980 when it permitted a brown and white shrimping season in the coastal areas in the spring and fall, respectively. These crustaceans are harvested in the canals on the leasehold by independent fishermen using specialized nets. The revenue hinges on the size of the catch and the prevailing local market price for shrimp. Although the income has fluctuated widely over the ten-year period the seasons have been open, from a low of $3,000 in 1980 to a high of $61,000 in 1988, the average annual $19,000 contribution has been significant to Vermilion's net income.

Vermilion has made other efforts to diversify the income from the lease operations but without success thus far. The corporation provided the acreage and some labor for an independent entrepreneur from Houston to operate an experimental catfish culture pond on ten acres of the leasehold in the Pecan Island area. After the required levee containment was constructed around the pond and water circulation, filtration, and drainage systems were installed, the pond was stocked in the fall of 1975 with catfish fingerlings and restocked in the spring of 1978.

Two harvests were taken from the pond, the last in early 1979, and produced excellent quality catfish meat but the yield in weight was disappointing and proved uneconomical. The owner-operator decided to terminate this experimental project, estimating his loss over the three and one-half year period to be about $20,000. He incurred all the costs, including construction of facilities, equipment purchases for the pond, high protein supplement feed, breedstock, and labor. Vermilion received about $3,200 for its share of the two harvests.

In the early 1980s, two other mariculture firms located in Texas were contacted and both expressed an interest in conducting surveys of the leasehold to determine its mariculture potential, using their qualified marine biologists and other technical personnel. In both cases, the charges for these surveys alone would have been prohibitive for Vermilion, so no further action was taken. With limited investment funds, Vermilion could not consider undertaking on its own the simplest of mariculture ventures, which are risky, both capital and labor intensive, and hold no guarantees of ultimate profitability.

In late 1986, the president of the domestic subsidiary of Sea Farm Inc., a Norwegian-based mariculture firm with diversified worldwide operations, initiated contact with Vermilion, expressing an interest in a survey of the property for three mariculture projects. He and technicians with his Company made a preliminary survey of the leasehold in early 1987 and were favorably impressed by the environmental conditions. However, no further action has been taken by Sea Farm, except to express an interest in establishing an alligator farm on the property at some time in the future.

* * *

In 1964, Vermilion and Humble negotiated, signed, and recorded in the records of Vermilion Parish a contract directly related to the surface lease under the formal caption "Committee Management Agreement By And Between Humble Oil & Refining Company And Vermilion Corporation" (hereinafter referred to as "the Agreement"). This document was to be a financial landmark in Vermilion's history. The income from certain defined sources other than Vermilion's lease operations to be shared in equal proportions between the two companies over subsequent years was to contribute to Vermilion's financial health in a way which has been inestimable. These shared revenues, initiated in that year, in large degree made possible the company's ability to pay annual dividends to its stockholders after 1966; to reward equitably its full-time employees; and to meet significant and continuing increases in many categories of expenditures year after year. The overall result was to provide recurring income and non-recurring income, diversifying the lease operations vested in Vermilion exclusively under the terms of the lease, many of which were highly cyclical from one year to the next, as indicated earlier.

Prior to entering this joint agreement, Humble and Vermilion had already shared revenues from certain types of non-lease income on an *ad hoc* 80 - 20 basis, respectively, during the years 1958-1963. These receipts were derived from a third-party trunk pipeline easement and damage payments.

By 1963, the two companies recognized that more such payments would be realized from third parties as a result of the Freshwater Bayou Canal, then under construction, from the grant of servitudes, easements, surface subleases, rights-of-way, and permits for the use of the private canals and waterways on the property. Representatives of both parties also recognized that the completion of the canal and its opening to public marine traffic would probably have a long-term, adverse impact on revenues derived from lease operations reserved to Vermilion.

Edmund McIlhenny, Louisiana legal counsel for Vermilion, had met with Harvey Condron, manager of Humble's Fee Land Management Department, at Belle Isle in late 1963 and reached an understanding on the basic terms of the agreement. McIlhenny then drafted the contract in February the following year for approval and signing by the two parties by April.

Under the terms of the agreement, a Joint Land Management Committee consisting of three persons was to be selected, one by Humble and two by Vermilion, to represent their respective views and interests. The original representatives for the latter were McIlhenny and Hebert, general manager of Vermilion, and both served until retirement in 1986 and 1972, respectively.

The Committee has the exclusive authority (subject to board approval in Vermilion's case) to review, approve and implement all subleases and grants of other commercial rights to third parties, provided only that unanimous approval is given by the three members. The revenues generated and all expenses incurred in the negotiations and legal documentation are to be shared by Humble and Vermilion equally or on a 50-50 basis.

Vermilion has had recurring income from sub-leases in every year since 1964 and non-recurring income in every year but 1976 from contracts signed with third parties with the approval of the Joint Committee. The first commercial land sublease was granted to Ocean Drilling & Exploration Company in 1964 and produced for Vermilion $1,200 in annual rental. Major long-term subleases, mentioned in Chapter One and still in operation, are the gas dehydration plant and barge terminal site of Columbia Gulf Transmission Company and Rip Tide Investors' marina and logistical support development known as Freshwater City below the lock on the west bank of the Freshwater Bayou Canal. The latter today is the major producer of shared income from subleases. The agreement for this sublease was signed and effective in June 1967 and lease payments are based on a fixed annual rental and a contingent percentage rental of the gross receipts generated annually.

Commercial land lease rentals expanded gradually over the first decade and one-half, from $1,200 to over $18,000 for Vermilion's portion in 1978. The record high of $70,000 in 1987 is about a 265% increase over the receipts of 1978 and obviously have become a major, high-ranking source of income for Vermilion.

The largest percentage of shared non-recurring income has been derived from pipeline easements (servitudes) and the balance from the occasional grants of other easements, permits for the use of the private canals and rights-of-way, such as the construction of the by-pass channel around the lock on Freshwater Bayou Canal for access to the Gulf of Mexico by the Sohio barges. Total shared revenue from all non-recurring sources has averaged just under $19,000 for the full thirty-one year period, with a low of less than $1,000 (excluding the year in which no revenue from this source was received) to a high of about $69,000 in 1979.

* * *

Another source of substantial revenue during the period 1984 through 1989 has been liquidated damages for seismic surveys conducted on the property for third parties. These payments, which have totaled more than $700,000, have been largely responsible for producing the strongest balance sheet in Vermilion's history. And they were fortuitous, considering the depressed conditions of domestic exploratory drilling during most of these years and the fact that the property was a "mature" area from the standpoint of geophysical exploration.[3] The receipt of this non-recurring income typifies the good fortune which has unexpectedly fallen in Vermilion's corporate lap through much of its history. Financial setbacks from declining, cyclical lease and other sources of revenue or from other causes have often been offset by new sources or sharp increases in some form of established revenues.

Finally, a new and recurring source of non-lease operating income was established in the second full year of Vermilion's history. Funds free of corporate working capital requirements have been invested in short-term and other appropriate securities over the three decades to partly counterbalance declines in other sources of revenue and continuing increases in corporate expenditures. During the first two decades, interest income was modest but nonetheless significant; however, it exceeded $10,000 in only five of these years. Over the past eleven years, total interest income has been over $207,000, averaging about $19,000 annually with a record high of about $62,000 in 1989.

In concluding this analysis of income sources and their evolution, it seems appropriate to take a retrospective view of gross receipts from all sources beginning with 1988, a milestone year in which Vermilion had over $1,000,000 for the first time in its history. This achievement would not have been possible without a confluence of record highs or near record highs in many lease and non-lease operations in addition to a substantial contribution from the new source of income from alligators eggs. These included hunting permits, land lease rentals, alligator and shrimping shares, damage payments from seismic operations, and investment income.

In the first full year of operations, gross income from all sources was about $65,000 and did not exceed $100,000 until 1965; $200,000 until 1974; and $500,000 until 1984. But with a few exceptions, the year-to-year trend was steadily upward throughout the thirty-one year period.

---

[3] It should be pointed out that the Gulf of Mexico since 1984 has become increasingly attractive for exploratory drilling from the standpoint of the potential for discovering sizable reserves in comparison with the forty-eight contiguous states. In addition, the political opposition of environmental and other groups has successfully blocked or delayed energy developments in other promising offshore areas of the United States and inland and offshore Alaska. Several of the seismic surveys conducted on the corporation's leasehold during this period may have been related to identifying promising new drilling prospects or those overlooked in the past offshore Vermilion Parish as well as inland.

CHAPTER VII

A HISTORIC VIEW OF THE EXPENSE SIDE OF THE LEDGER AND THE "BOTTOM LINE"

To understand Vermilion's consistent profitability in relation to its rapidly growing expenditures over the past two decades, it is necessary to place in perspective its transformed corporate character in relation to its two predecessors; the expansion of the lease operations from the first year; most notably, the growth of sources of revenue shared equally with Humble/Exxon since 1964; the growth of interest income; and the substantial receipts for surface damages from seismic operations over the past six years.

Unlike Furs, Inc., and Furs Corp., Vermilion is a labor intensive corporation rather than capital intensive. At the time of dissolution in 1958, Furs Corp. had capital assets of $618,000, including investments in the landholding of $573,000 and the balance in depreciated building facilities and furnishings at Belle Isle and boats, marsh buggies, dredging and other equipment. Resident management and a few employees were part-time, except during the hunting and trapping seasons from November through mid-February.

In contrast, Vermilion had no investment in the leasehold; inherited the facilities in place at Belle Isle with a long-term maintenance responsibility; and, as noted earlier, purchased the equipment, furnishings, and moveable facilities at a depreciated fair market value. The lease operations as expanded over the years were all labor intensive requiring expanded full- and part-time personnel, including management oversight.

In addition, Vermilion acts as a service organization for Bayou members and guests for the migratory wildfowl hunting season for about two months of the year. Most of the hours of the full-time staff of officers and employees is devoted to discharging the service obligations defined in the hunting sublease during this period and beyond until the final invoice of compensable services is completed. Part-time employees are hired during the season, such as guides, cooks, and housekeeping personnel. The daily usage of the Belle Isle facilities by Bayou members and guests has risen substantially over the past two decades, particularly in comparison to the usage by the officers and other directors of Furs Corp. and Furs, Inc. How-

Expense Side of the Ledger 65

ever, the usage has declined substantially from the peak year of 1987 because of the shortened hunting seasons and the lower bag limits mandated by regulatory agencies.

Finally, the expanded lease operations, maintenance and repair of buildings and equipment, and projects for preservation of the environment have become year-round responsibilities, requiring a larger full-time work force.

From the outset of Vermilion's operations, wage and salary payments were by far the largest expense, ranging from a low of 41.5 percent of the total in 1960 to a high of 50.4 percent in 1965. In one other year—1968—this item also exceeded 50 percent of the total. Over the first decade, wages and salaries remained relatively stable, averaging about $30,000 annually, and then accelerated with the expansion of the lease and other operations until they had almost doubled by 1974 to $59,000. After 1974, this expenditure accelerated at a much higher rate, from $79,700 in 1975 to $288,900 in 1989. There were substantial percentage increases from one year to the next, with only two exceptions, varying from a high of 29.7 percent in 1980 over 1979 to a low of 6.6% in 1985 over 1984. The two declines were registered in 1986 and 1989 and were less than one percentage point.

Rising wage and salary expenditures are attributed to a number of factors, including long-range inflationary pressures on the cost of living; minimum wage increases; the expansion of the full-time staff and part-time employees to handle diversified operations and increasing liaison with government agencies and private organizations; the establishment of new management positions; and the conversion of top resident management to full-time from part-time.[1]

Until 1971, the annual lease rental of $5,000 ranked a low second in the expense ledger.[2] Excepting the non-recurring special expenses for legal fees, total insurance premiums for all types of coverage replaced the annual rental as a rapidly rising expense item and has become a major cost burden for Vermilion, exceeding $108,000 in the years 1988-1989. Beginning in 1973, the year-to-year percentage increase was geometrical with a 31 percent rise in that year over 1972 and 22.7, 22.4, and 29.2 percent in the following three years. The record high was a 51 percent increase in 1979 over 1978. In only one year to the present was the increase less than

---

[1] The expansion of the full-time staff will be discussed in Chapter IX.

[2] The non-cash outlay for depreciation is excluded from the ranking of expense items.

double digit, with only two declines in the period which were a minuscule percentage.

These quantum leaps in insurance costs have applied to casualty, property damage, liability and health coverage. And Vermilion is particularly vulnerable because its buildings and equipment are located in a low lying coastal area subject to periodic tropical storms and hurricanes. Moreover, it has heavy exposure to marine liability and casualty premiums which are rated high-risk by insurers. Excepting the state road across the leasehold and the impractical use of helicopters, access to Belle Isle and many other sectors of the property and the hunting blinds and areas by employees and Bayou members is limited to marine transport. Insurance premiums over the years 1988 and 1989 have averaged 17 percent of total expenditures and ten percent and higher since 1985.

In 1982 and subsequent years, the annual lease rental and additional contingent rental obligation incurred returned to a strong third place in expense ranking, after Vermilion and Exxon negotiated a compromise settlement of a controversy over this payment (see Chapter VIII). The terms of the settlement were recorded as an amendment to the surface lease and resulted in a 440 percent increase in the first year of application in 1982, from $5,000 or Vermilion's interpretation of the obligation prior to the settlement of the controversy to over $27,000. Over the following seven-year period from 1983 through 1989, the average base and additional contingent lease rental has been about $35,000 with a high of $46,300 in 1988.

Aside from wages and salaries, insurance premiums and the lease rental (after 1981), other operating expenses have generally reflected the consumer price inflationary trend over the past three decades.

Total operating expenses were relatively stable over the first thirteen years from 1959 through 1971, averaging annually about $70,000. The total rose rapidly in 1972 and in every year thereafter with the exception of a decline of less than five percent in 1989 compared to 1988. Expenses in 1972 exceeded $100,000 for the first time, or a twenty percent increase over the prior year. The year 1973 marked the first of continuing dramatic increases in insurance premiums and was followed by a major restructuring to full-time resident management in 1980, with a concomitant increase in salaries.

The low of total expenses of $57,600 in 1963 advanced to an all-time high in 1988 of $648,600, reflecting the expansion of operations and service requirements as well as a high percentage of uncontrollable costs, such as insurance premiums and the annual lease rental.

Expense Side of the Ledger 67

* * *

Whether Vermilion could have survived on the income from the lease operations alone, as defined in the surface lease and amended in 1959, is a moot question, at least when applied to the early years. Presenting his historical perspective of the organizational period in a memorandum dated June 1981, McBride expressed the concern as follows:

> Stripped of royalties as a result of the merger of Louisiana Furs into Humble, Adams and I seriously questioned whether or not Vermilion could be viable based on the operations covered by the Lease. This fear was translated into budget projections which anticipated losses for several years.

John Donohue, then treasurer and auditor for Vermilion, emphasized the same point in an analysis of income statements which covered a brief period in fiscal 1958 and the two following years:

> From the above comparisons of Vermilion's operating statements, it can be seen that were it not for the substantial amount of easements and damages collected from the pipeline and oil companies, totaling $57,638.54 over the three-year span, Vermilion's operations would have resulted in a total deficit of $37,226.82 instead of the present earned surplus of $16,482.20.

After deducting commercial land lease rentals from the annual income statements—a shared item of income with Humble/Exxon beginning in 1964—Vermilion would have had deficits on lease operations alone for seventeen out of thirty-one years of operations through fiscal 1989, resulting in a net deficit of $37,000.

In any event, the so-called "bottom line" on the financial statement of income and expenses has been a profit of some magnitude in all thirty-one years of Vermilion's history through fiscal 1989, ranging from a per share low of $0.02 in 1963 to a record high of $21.15 in 1988. The year 1982 was in fact a large deficit year, because of the settlement of the lease rental controversy which required a payment to Exxon of $75,000 for the cumulative contingent rental owing for prior years. This sum was charged against retained earnings as a tax-loss carry-forward which left operations in the black for that year, even with the additional contingent rental payment.

Obviously, the record of profitability has depended heavily on the shared income with Humble/Exxon under the land management agreement signed in 1964, recurring and non-recurring; and other non-recurring income from surface damage reimbursements, although in four of the years since 1980 lease operations alone have made sizable after-tax contributions.

CHAPTER VIII

THE EXXON - VERMILION CONTINGENT LEASE RENTAL CONTROVERSY AND ITS SETTLEMENT

In mid-1980, at the regular meeting of the Vermilion board, Lloyd McBride notified the directors that Rex Patrick and Hubert Smith, the manager and deputy manager of Exxon's Fee Land Management Department, had received Vermilion's audited financial statements from the beginning of operations and raised the issue of overdue contingent rental for most of these years. McBride expressed the opinion at the time that a "position paper" with the historical aspects of the grant of the surface lease by Furs Corporation to Vermilion would clarify the interpretation of certain terminology of the base and additional rental considerations. He also believed that the controversy would not have a major adverse financial impact on Vermilion.

Negotiations on this matter were to continue until the resolution in November 1982 or a period of more than two years.[1] Closely related to the settlement and the only other serious legal problem Vermilion has confronted in its history was litigation over several years involving the successful defense of its control over the use of the private canals on the leasehold. This matter was resolved in 1981. Exxon adjusted its final terms of settlement for the back contingent lease rental by one-half of the approximate $62,000 in legal fees which Vermilion had expended on this litigation, recognizing that the case was in the mutual interest of both lessor and lessee.

The core issue in the lease rental controversy was the interpretation of the language in the original surface lease on the rental payment. The minimum annual base rental was fixed at $5,000.00, and

> If during any calendar year beginning with the year 1959 the gross income received by Lessee . . . shall exceed Fifty Thousand & No/100 ($50,000) Dollars, Lessee shall . . . pay Lessor as addi-

---

[1] One of the reasons for this protracted period before settlement was the serious illness which afflicted McBride in the midst of the negotiations and which required frequent hospitalizations.

tional rental for such year an amount which when added to the Five Thousand & No/100 ($5,000.00) Dollars will total ten (10%) percent of gross income received by Lessee.

In 1979, when this issue was raised by Exxon representatives, gross income from lease operations reserved to Vermilion had reached $206,000. There were other conflicting views between the two parties, such as the treatment of Bayou's compensable services as an entry under the income side of the financial statement and Bayou's annual rental for the Hunting Sublease, but these were marginal to the core issue or the definition of "gross income."

McBride was a principal in the organization of Vermilion and Bayou and he also drafted the surface lease granted to Vermilion by Furs Corp. before its dissolution. Apart from his extensive corporate legal experience, he was the only person with direct knowledge about the true intent of the original parties to the agreements and obviously became the sole negotiator for Vermilion throughout the protracted period leading to the compromise settlement. Although he offered compromise proposals to the Exxon representatives, he maintained throughout the negotiations that, "however ill-chosen the term 'gross income' might be in retrospect, the intent was 'Net Income' . . ." In further elaboration, he stated:

> It is Vermilion's position that the term means 'Net Income' or, at the very most 'Net Operating Income' . . . based on the original intent of the parties and as supported by subsequent acts and facts emerging from Vermilion's operations and from the expanded operating relationship between Humble/Exxon and Vermilion.[2] 2

Patrick and Smith, representing Exxon, held firmly to the position that "gross income" was a well-defined and established accounting term and "is an all-inclusive figure which represents total revenue . . . ," converted to net income only after deductions.

In the effort to reach a compromise, McBride prepared three documents over the approximate two and one-half years of negotiations, with assistance from John Donohue in presenting attached exhibits and schedules of adjusted financial data on the rental computation over the years 1959 through 1980. One of the exhibits highlighted Vermilion's heavy dependence on non-lease operating income for profitability over this entire period:

---

[2] McBride, *Exxon-Vermilion Surface Lease: Rental Computation* (June 22, 1981), pp.8-9.

Of these total earnings of $537,681, only a net of $15,394 was contributed from sources covered by the Lease as computed under Exhibit 'A' (13 years for a total loss of $95,805 and 10 years for a total profit of $111,199).

McBride made a final proposal which partly accepted Exxon's interpretation of "gross income" but this was rejected. Essentially, he proposed that different percentage brackets be applied to three different categories of gross lease operating revenue totals: hunting leases, pasturing income, and trapping combined with all other sources, five percent up to and including $100,000; six percent from over $100,000 up to and including $150,000; and seven percent for revenues in excess of $150,000.

Before and after this documentation of Vermilion's position was prepared, there were three direct negotiating sessions among the representatives of the two parties. Patrick and Smith met with McBride in Chicago in September 1980; and Patrick returned for a second meeting with McBride in Chicago in January 1982. McBride had a final session with Patrick in Houston in August 1982, before preparing his final memorandum with the above proposal, dated October 7, 1982.

What appeared to be Exxon's final offer in settlement of the additional rental claimed to be owing for the years 1959 through 1981 and for other rental adjustments, dated October 19, 1982, carried a short deadline for acceptance and proposed the following terms for amendment of the surface lease.

1) Exxon would accept a payment of $75,000 for additional rental owing for the years 1959 through 1981, a substantial reduction from its initial claim. Without obligation to do so, Exxon had taken into account as a part of the reduction the approximate $30,000 or one-half of Vermilion's litigation fees in the canal trespass case.

2) Exxon identified specifically all income received by Vermilion in the future which would be exempt from the additional rental percentage.

3) Exxon granted a lower percentage on the additional rental obligation, reducing it from ten percent to eight percent, with the base minimum rental of $5,000 applying to the first $75,000 of gross income, compared to the original minimum of $50,000.

On receipt of this offer, McBride convened an informal meeting of the Vermilion board at Belle Isle on November 13, 1982, with all but two directors able to attend. After a full discussion of the proposed compromise settlement and its ramifications, the directors unanimously voted to support the terms and pledged their future votes at the annual meeting in December when the action was placed in the formal records of the company.

The payment for the back additional lease rental was forwarded promptly to Exxon and the amended surface lease was signed by qualified officers of both parties by the end of November. Fortunately, both Exxon and Vermilion were determined from the outset to resolve the controversy without resort to litigation, if possible, and had no disagreement on that issue.

At the annual meeting of the Vermilion board in December 1982, the directors passed a resolution commending McBride for his protracted efforts to obtain the best possible solution. The central concern for all directors during the negotiations was a settlement under a lease rental formula with which Vermilion could remain viable into the future and continue to progress financially.

From Exxon's standpoint, their representatives had every obligation to their stockholders to impose the conventional definition of "gross income" in a way which did not lead to the Lessee's inability to survive as a corporate entity. During the negotiations, Exxon representatives made clear that they did not want to have any participation in Vermilion's conduct of lease operations.

Exxon also granted some substantial concessions in its final offer, particularly the lowering of the additional rental percentage, a substantial reduction in its original claim for back additional rental and recognition that Bayou's payments for compensable services were a reimbursement at cost to Vermilion. However, Exxon did not exempt Bayou's annual lease rental payment to Vermilion from the total of gross lease income, an objective which McBride sought on grounds that it was an "intracorporate payment."

The major problem which McBride confronted at the outset of negotiations was acceptance of the original intent of the parties; that is, they intended "net income before taxes" rather than "gross income." If any principal or principals of Humble had been available to verify this intent, perhaps the final outcome would have been somewhat different. But this is speculation, given Exxon's firm adherence to the conventional definition of "gross income."

CHAPTER IX

OWNERSHIP, MANAGEMENT, STAFF AND ADMINISTRATION: PRINCIPAL CHANGES OVER THREE DECADES

From its origins to the present, the composition of Vermilion's board of directors, full- and part-time officers and ownership reflect a remarkable continuity in the descendants of the families involved with the Gulf Coast Club and Coast Land, described at the close of Chapter II. At least until recent years, changes have been infrequent and resulted from either death or retirement.

Ownership stability is attributable to a number of factors. Perhaps most important, deceased stockholders have made their descendants or surviving spouses beneficiaries of Vermilion shares, with occasional exceptions, over many decades. Apart from the probable family sentimental attachment in many cases, the inheritors obviously had no direct investment in these bequests.

At first glance, it might be concluded that ownership continuity was partly determined by the absence of any conventional auction or principal/agent markets for the shares, limiting buyers and sellers largely to the 90 or less stockholders. This apparently has not been the case.

Without any legal obligation to review this matter, the Vermilion board recognized that it could pose a potential problem, particularly for owners of a small number of shares seeking to liquidate them. There was no facile and equitable solution. Finally, in December 1988, the directors approved a Share Repurchase Program for owners with fewer than 100 shares at a price of book value at the close of fiscal 1988, reduced by the dividend payable the following January. Only four eligible stockholders tendered a total of 181 shares under the program offer which was open for sixty days and expired without extension on April 1, 1989.

Another factor in the stability of ownership is the small capitalization of Vermilion, which has varied a maximum of 1,122 shares issued and outstanding throughout its history, from a high of 12,657 shares during 1971-1975 to a low of 11,535 in 1980, a variance of less than nine percent. In addition, Vermilion has seldom granted options to purchase shares and only when these were held in treasury from infrequent purchases of shares outstanding. Since 1980, however, the board established a policy of granting share purchase options to new directors who did not own shares, or owned fewer than 200 shares, to buy up to that amount at book value when available in treasury.[1]

Combining all of the factors above with the unique characteristics of the leasehold and lease operations leads to the conclusion that a large percentage of the owners regards Vermilion as a rare multi-family type of corporation and investment asset.

* * *

The composition of the board of directors during the first twenty-two years, from 1958 until late 1980, was unusually stable. Over this period, four of the original directors died, including Richard Baldwin, the president since 1958, and two decided not to stand for reelection. As of December 1980, Lloyd McBride and Dan Peterkin, Jr., were the last of the charter directors to continue in active service on the board, Pat Adams having retired on that date; and only four directors had been elected as replacements.

Far more frequent changes have occurred over the past nine years. Seven new directors have been elected since December 1980; three directors have died; and three decided not to stand for reelection. Adams (until his death in February 1990), Edmund McIlhenny, Sr., Scott Probasco, Jr. and Sunny Westfeldt, Jr. continue to maintain their association with the board after retirement as directors emeritus.

Over the thirty-one years, the board membership has varied from six to a high of ten, but the largest number applied only to a brief period in December 1983. The Executive Committee, composed of three members and empowered to act on behalf of the Board on most decisions between annual and regular (semi-annual) meetings, has had a total of only eight different incumbents during this period.[2]

Except for the special organizational meetings in 1958, Vermilion held only annual meetings of directors at the hunting lodge on Belle Isle, continuing the practice of Furs, Inc., and Furs Corp. This was a convenience

---

[1] Share ownership of course is not a requirement under Vermilion By-Laws to serve as a director or officer of the Corporation.

[2] Appendix A provides the composition and chronology of service of the Board of Directors and Executive Committee.

Ownership, Management, Staff

and also a cost saving practice, since all directors—until 1964—were Bayou Members and could usually schedule their hunting to coincide with the Vermilion meetings date or November each year, the same timing of the Bayou meetings.

One of three major administrative changes occurred in 1969, when a regular meeting was scheduled in addition to the annual meeting to maintain a more frequent review of the expanded operations; and the location was changed to Chicago in order to provide a greater separation from Bayou's meetings and activities. The only exception to the Chicago site until 1984, was the informal session convened by McBride in November 1982 at Belle Isle in order to meet the short deadline in response to Exxon's proposal for settlement of the contingent rental controversy.

Apart from the Joint Humble - Vermilion Land Management Agreement of 1964, discussed earlier, the only other major administrative change was made by the board after McBride's death in December 1983. Beginning in June 1984, all annual stockholder and director annual and regular meetings have been held in Houston. Circumstances had substantially altered at that juncture to make the new location far more convenient from a travel standpoint with an accompanying substantial reduction in meeting expenses. (One director was a Houston resident in 1984 and in 1988 three directors were residents of this city.) In addition, the board consolidated the administrative and operating offices in Abbeville and canceled Vermilion's certificate of qualification for operations in the state of Illinois.

The officers of Vermilion, including the full-time resident management, have had extended incumbency, providing a stability and continuity to operational oversight similar to that of the board and ownership. The same applies to other resident employees. There have been three presidents since 1958, with Baldwin serving by far the longest period of 22 years, followed by Frank Knapp, Jr., who served eight years until elected to the newly created post of chairman in 1988 when Donohue was elected president.

Other officers, their positions and tenure are as follows: vice president: Dan Peterkin, Jr., 1958-1988 (with senior rank); J. Mark Hebert, 1958-1972; John P. Donohue, 1972-1988; and Edmund McIlhenny, Jr., 1988 to the present; secretaries: Lloyd McBride, 1958-1983; Donohue, 1984-1988; McIlhenny, Jr., 1988 to the present; treasurer: Donohue, 1958 to the present; general counsel, McBride, 1958-1983; and Louisiana counsel, Edmund McIlhenny, Sr., 1959-1986.

The chief operating officer of Vermilion, as was true of the two predecessor companies, is the resident general manager, who now has a variety of responsibilities in addition to the general oversight of lease and non-lease operations. These include selection of new personnel and review of the performance of all members of the full-time staff; identifying and recommending conservation projects and other major capital expenditures; liaison with private organizations, such as the National Alligator Association; and liaison and negotiations with federal, state and local governmental regulatory agencies with approval and permit authority over conservation projects and other uses of the property.

The general manager is also *ex offico* one of the two Vermilion members of the Exxon-Vermilion Joint Land Management Committee which holds authority over approval of non-lease commercial grants on the leasehold.

J. Mark Hebert, who began his service under Dr. R. O. Young with Furs, Inc., in 1927, replaced Young as resident manager in the mid-1940s and served Vermilion as general manager until his retirement in 1972. He initiated the sale of hunting lease permits outside the area reserved to Bayou in the first year of operations, a source of income which in recent years has ranked by far as the highest contributor among single sources of lease and non-lease operations.[3]

Donohue replaced Hebert in 1972 and continues in this capacity to the present. Although initially this was a part-time position supplementing his accounting practice, his duties and responsibilities almost from the outset were much broader than those of his predecessor. By 1980, they had expanded to the point that the position could only be handled on a full-time basis, as noted below. Donohue has held every officer position of Vermilion, excepting the recently created chairman, assistants and legal counsel, and since 1972 has not held less than three at any one time.[4]

Among other full- and part-time employees, the key position has generally been that of field superintendant, which was held by Murphy ("Red") Sellers for about 45 years with Vermilion and its predecessors

---

[3] Mark Hebert had almost 45 years of continuous service with Furs, Inc., Furs Corp. and Vermilion.

[4] John Donohue is the only living and active original officer of Vermilion Corporation. During the organization and meeting of Vermilion in August 1958, the newly established board of directors authorized J. E. Kibbe and Mark Hebert to select an accountant from a firm in the Abbeville area to perform bookkeeping and auditing of financial statements and the accountant selected would *ipso facto* serve as treasurer of Vermilion. Donohue was interviewed by Kibbe for the position and accepted this assignment.

until his retirement in late 1987. This position entails the day-to-day supervision of the full- and part-time personnel connected with the lease operations and the services provided by Vermilion to Bayou under the terms of the hunting sublease during the migratory wildfowl season lasting about 70 days each year. Among the various duties of resident personnel are maintenance and repair of boats, hunting and specialized marsh and other equipment; dredging, levee maintenance and other conservation projects; maintenance and repair of facilities at Belle Isle; patrolling against trespassing and poaching; providing marine transportation for Bayou members and guests; and accounting for the size of the harvests of alligators, fur-bearing animals and shrimp, fishing and crayfish shares.

In April 1987, William Wainwright III was employed as field foreman in anticipation of Sellers' retirement. For fourteen years, he had been the resident manager and chief guide of a smaller land company near the Vermilion leasehold with some hunting and other operations similar to those of Vermilion.

Many of the full- and part-time employees of Vermilion and predecessors have served extended periods of time and some of their offspring or relatives have continued their employment traditions with Vermilion. For example, Evince Guidry, who retired at the same time as Sellers in 1987, had a service record of over fifty years.

A major management change occurred in 1980 when the board approved the election of Donohue to full-time general manager with the provisoes that he phase out his accounting practice as soon as convenient to the clientele and employ a qualified candidate to serve as assistant general manager under him. William P. Edwards, III, with educational specialities and experience in land and wildlife management and environmental conservation, was employed in this capacity in July 1980 and subsequently has been elected to the additional position of assistant secretary.

EPILOGUE:
A BRIEF GLANCE BACKWARD AND FORWARD

Vermilion's history dates back to 1924 with the organization of the Coast Land Company. This company and each of the three successors are in reality a historical chapter in a single book with the fourth open and continuing until the year 2057 under the terms of the Vermilion leasehold. As this brief monograph has attempted to emphasize, there have been many areas of unique continuity throughout the combined sixty-six years of operations—owners, officers, directors, resident management and employees, the enjoyment of sports hunting, and the development of the facilities for this activity. The land with its produce from minerals, farming, fishing, hunting and trapping also continued as the most valuable asset of all four companies.

But there have been a number of striking and radical changes, particularly over the past twenty-four years, that did not characterize Vermilion's earlier years. Several new sources of revenue developed unexpectedly, many of a sizable magnitude relative to Vermilion's first years of income and to that of its predecessors. With the possible exception of investment income and the income from sources shared with Humble/Exxon in 1964 and later years, management was not in the position to promote any of these sources of revenue and had no control over their timing. To the contrary, grants or subleases were sought by third parties; and governmental regulatory bodies permitted new lease operations, such as the harvest of alligators, the two shrimping seasons and the sale of alligator eggs to licensed commercial alligator farm operators.

In addition, the relative size of the expanded lease operations have fluctuated dramatically over the years. As noted earlier, trapping was by far the largest of three surface operations during the era of Furs, Inc., and Furs Corp. and was a major source of income for Vermilion for most of the first three decades of operations. In fiscal 1989, trapping shares were by far the smallest contributor to gross income, producing a minuscule amount and with bleak prospects for recovery. Management has little control over these fluctuations, which are determined by the vagaries of market prices, weather and other environmental factors, consumer demand and changing rules of various federal, state and local regulatory agencies.

Finally, it should also be noted that the reorganizations of 1952 and 1958 were not mere changes in the corporation names but fundamental

Epilogue

restructurings under the newly organized corporations, Furs Corp. and Vermilion.

In looking forward, it would appear superficially that the results of lease operations would be relatively easy to forecast, but this is not the case except for three mature and stable operations—grazing, rice shares and fishing/crayfish shares. The revenues from these sources are likely to average in the future close to the average of the past ten years.

The linchpin of lease operations in the years ahead will continue to be hunting lease rentals which are now in a mature stage at current income levels. The drought of 1988 and the restrictions on bag limits of migratory wildfowl and reduction of the length of the hunting season by federal and state regulatory agencies suggest some of the hazards of forecasting lease operating income even from one of the most reliable sources. Moreover, the migratory wildlife population on the property has been in a long-term decline over many years after the construction of the Freshwater Bayou Canal and the adverse effects on the habitat. In the meanwhile, other refuge areas have been opened along the flight paths of migratory wildfowl from Canada.

Future results of other major lease operations—alligator shares, alligator egg sales and shrimping shares—have either fluctuated too widely in recent years or are yet unestablished as a recurring source of revenue (in the case of the second category) to forecast long-range trends. All depend on current market prices and the first two categories also depend on the supply of, and demand for, alligator hides and finished products.

Over time, the increase in supply of alligator hides from the production of commercial farms in Louisiana and Florida, combined with the natural harvests permitted by state agencies, could have an adverse effect on the price per foot. And, in Louisiana, the potential increase of the alligator population in the natural habitats from the required seventeen percent replacement of surviving hatchlings from the eggs removed for alligator farm incubation could lead to increased quotas for landowners for the natural harvest, also reducing prices per foot.

One prognostication for the future can be made almost categorically. Expenditures are likely to rise, although probably not by the high percentage, year-to-year increases since 1982 from the lease rental amendment and insurance premiums. Two sources of recurring income are available to offset in part the annual expense increases expected to materialize— investment income and land lease rentals. The latter are expected to increase moderately until 1996, even if no additional subleases are granted between the present and that year.

Returning to the past, it is interesting to compare and repeat the forecasts of three key figures in the history of Vermilion and its predecessors. McBride and Adams at the time of Vermilion's formation strongly believed that it would face several years of deficit operations. All the comparative financial data available at that time supported and justified their conclusion. However, with the good fortune of receiving totally unanticipated income from new sources from the start of corporate operations, Vermilion was profitable in every year to the present, excepting 1982. In that year, the contingent rental controversy was settled and the payment made to Exxon for the rental owing for prior years.

In an earlier era, at the time of the formation of Louisiana Furs, Inc., in late 1927, Dr. R. O. Young selected this corporate name over Vermilion because of the then prevailing local legend that any business enterprise with the latter title would not be successful. Thus far into its history, Vermilion has buried this myth which may no longer be remembered by the local population.

APPENDIX A

SUBSCRIBERS TO THE STOCK OF LOUISIANA COAST LAND COMPANY
(as of September 1925)

Name	No. Shares (@ $2,000 each)	Residence	Occupation/Position
Adams, Walter	5	St. Louis	Pres. Adams Net & Twine Co.
Alexander, C. H.	1	N.A.[1]*	N.A.
Bell, James F.[2]**	5	Minneapolis	V. P. Washburn-Crosby Co.
Billings, Frank**	1	Chicago	Physician
Billings, C. K. G.	1	N.A.	N.A.
Branigar, W. W.	5	N.A.	N.A.
Carroll, Paul	5	Marquette, MI	N.A.
Clement, Allan M.	5	Chicago	Pres. Clement, Curtis & Co.
Couch, Ira J.	1	N.A.	N.A.
Cowles, Alfred	4	Chicago	"Capitalist"
Dickinson, B. M.	5	Pittsburgh	Physician
Garrett, Lewis F.	5	N.A.	N.A.
Hammers, Morgan J.	5	Chicago	Pres. Nokol Co.
Hay, H. Collins	1	Chicago	Attor./Partner, Synder & Hay
Hedges, M. M.	5	Chattanooga	Pres. Casey-Hedges Co.
Johnson, E. R.	5	Camden, NJ	Pres. Victor Talking Mach. Co.
Joyce, Edward J.	5	Chicago	Pres. Joyce Filing Co.
Knight, Harry F.	5	St. Louis	Pres. Knight, Gamble, Goddard
LaBahn, Paul O.	5	Chicago	Hallbauer-LaBahn, Inc.
Marland, E. W.	33	Ponca City, OK	Pres. Marland Oil Co.
Meehan, G. F.	5	Chattanooga	Pres. Ross-Meehan Foundries
Moller, A. W.	5	New York City	Pres. The Duz Co.
Morton, Joy	5	Chicago	Pres. Morton Salt Co.
Murray, J. C.	1	N.A.	N.A.
McCally, J. C.	5	Chicago	Attorney
McCormick, Cyrus H.	3	Chicago	McCormick Harvester Co.
McCrea, W. S.**	1	Chicago	"Sportsman and Capitalist"
McFadden, W. H.	34	Ponca City, OK	Vice Pres. Marland Oil Co.
McIlhenny, E. A.	20	Avery Island	Pres. McIlhenny Co.
Mills, W. McM.	1	New York City	Pes. Central Union Trust Co.
Penton, John A.	5	Cleveland	Pres. Penton Publishing Co.
Perera, G. L.	1	N.A.	N.A.
Playfair, James	1	Midland-Canada	Pres. Great Lakes Trans. Ltd.
Poppenhusen, C. H.	4	Chicago	N.A.
Probasco, Scott L.	N.A.	Chattanooga	Pres. Amer. Bank & Trust Co.
Rand, J. O.	5	N.A.	N.A.

* Not Available

** Members of the Louisiana Gulf Coat Club Advisory Board

Smith, Sidney	5	Chicago	N.A.
Smith, Z. E.	5	Chicago	Architect
Smith, D. B.	5	N.A.	N.A.
Steedman, Edwin H.	5	St. Louis	Pres. Curtis Manuf. Co.
Stewart, Philip B.	1	N.A.	N.A.
Strom, George A.	1	N.A.	N.A.
Vilas, R. C.	4	Chicago	Pres. Pyle National Co.
Vilas Trust	5	---------	---------------
Vilas, L. H.	5	N.A.	N.A.
Warick, W. E.	5	Chicago	V. P. Standard Oil of IN
Watkins, Horton	5	St. Louis	V. P. International Shoe Co.
Wright, Warren	5	Chicago	Pres. Calumet Baking Powder Co.
Young, Edward J.	1	N.A.	N.A.

APPENDIX B

CHRONOLOGICAL COMPOSITION OF THE BOARD OF DIRECTORS AND EXECUTIVE COMMITTEE OF VERMILION CORPORATION

* Indicates death or retirement
** Indicates a newly elected Director during the beginning year of the period

BOARD OF DIRECTORS

1958-1959
Richard Baldwin	Clayton J. Adams	Daniel Peterkin, Jr.
David A. Wallace	Scott L. Probasco, Sr.*	Lloyd M. McBride
Frank A. Knapp, Sr.	(died 1959)	George A. Lyon, Jr.

1959-1962
Baldwin	Adams	Peterkin, Jr.
Wallace*	Probasco, Jr.**	McBride
(d. 1962)	Knapp, Sr.	Lyon, Jr. (retired)

1962-1964
Baldwin	Adams	Peterkin, Jr.
Knapp, Sr.*	Probasco, Jr.	McBride
(d. 1963)		Edmund McIlhenny, Sr.**

1964-1976
Baldwin	Peterkin, Jr.	Knapp, Jr.**
Adams	McBride	
Probasco, Jr.	McIlhenny, Sr.	

1976-1980
Baldwin*	Peterkin, Jr.	John P. Donohue**
(d. 1980)	McBride	Probasco, Jr.
Adams	McIlhenny, Sr.	Knapp, Jr.

1980-1983
Edwin S. Baldwin**	Peterkin, Jr.	Donohue
Adams*	McBride	Probasco, Jr.
(retired)	(d. 1983)	Knapp, Jr.
Walter McIlhenny**	George Westfeldt, Jr.**	Edmund McIlhenny, Sr.

83

1983-1985
W. McIlhenny   Peterkin, Jr.   Probasco, Jr.**
E. Baldwin   Westfeldt, Jr.   (retired)
E. McIlhenny, Sr.   Donohue   Knapp, Jr.
                                              Oral L. Luper**

1985-1986
E. McIlhenny, Sr.*   Westfeldt, Jr.*   Peterkin, Jr.
(retired 1986)   (retired 1986)   Donohue
E. McIlhenny, Jr.**   Knapp, Jr.   Luper
W. McIlhenny*   Nelson Jones**
(d. 1985)
E. Baldwin

1986-1988
E. Baldwin   Donohue   Knapp, Jr.
E. McIlhenny, Jr.   Luper
Peterkin, Jr.*   Jones
(d. 1988)

1988-present
E. Baldwin   Donohue   Knapp, Jr.
E. McIlhenny, Jr.   Luper
Ken E. Montague**   Jones

Executive Committee

1958-1963	R. Baldwin	Clayton J. Adams	Knapp, Sr.*
1963-1980	R. Baldwin*	Adams*	E. McIlhenny, Sr.
1980-1984	Knapp, Jr.	McBride*	E. McIlhenny, Sr.
1984-1986	Knapp, Jr.	Donohue	E. McIlhenny, Sr.
1986-present	Knapp, Jr.	Donohue	E. McIlhenny, Jr.**

Index

Abbeville, La., 2, 22, 24, 26, 27, 43, 54, 75
Acadia Parish, La., 8
Adams, Clayton J. "Pat," 19, 20, 32, 38, 41, 43, 67, 74, 80, 83, 84
Adams, Walter, 81
Alexander, C. H., 81
American Banking & Trust Company, 14, 22
American National Bank and Trust Company, 22
Audubon Society, see National Audubon Society
Avery Island, La., 8, 14, 27

Baldwin, Edwin S., 22, 83, 84
Baldwin, Richard, 20, 22, 38, 43, 75, 83
Bank of Abbeville, 35
Bayou Corporation, 5, 21, 24, 41, 42, 55, 66, 70, 72
Bayou Reserved Area, 41
Bell, James F., 81
Belle Isle Bayou, 3
Belle Isle Canal, 3
Belle Isle, La., 5, 20, 26, 33, 41, 61, 62, 66, 71, 74
Big Game Grounds, 8
Billings, C. K. G., 81
Billings, Frank, 81
Branigar, W. W., 81

Canyonlands National Park, 54
Carroll, Paul, 81
Chattanooga, Tenn., 14, 22
Chicago Title & Trust Co., 10
Chicago, Ill., 10, 14, 18, 26, 47, 71, 75
Chrysler Corporation, 24
Clement, Allan M., 81
Columbia Gulf Transmission Company, 4, 5, 62
Condron, Harvey, 61
Couch, Ira J., 81
Cowles, Alfred, 81
Curtice, Harlow, 24
Curtis Manufacturing Company, 14, 21

Dees, Theodore A., 6
Detroit, Mich., 24
Dickinson, B. M., 81
Donohue and Poché, 43
Donohue, John, 43, 67, 75, 76, 77, 83
Dymond, John, Jr., 10

Edwards, William P. III, 54
Exchange Oil Company, 5
Exxon Corporation, 41, 53, 55, 66-72, 75

First Mortgage Bondholders, 16, 17, 22
Fort Worth, Texas, 23
Freshwater Bayou Canal, 3-5, 45, 48, 50-53, 61, 62
Freshwater Bayou, 3, 46, 49
Freshwater City, La., 5, 62

G. C. Alligator Farm, 59
Garrett, Lewis F., 81
General Motors Corporation, 24
Grand Chenier, La., 4, 59
Guidry, Evince, 77

Hammers, Morgan J., 14, 17, 25, 30, 38, 81
Hay, H. Collins, 14, 81
Hebert, J. Mark, 23, 25, 27, 32, 38, 61, 75, 76
Hedges, M. M., 81
Hibernia Bank and Trust Company, 15, 16
Houston, Tex., 71, 75
Humble Oil and Refining Co., x, xii, 21, 31, 32, 40-42, 53, 55, 60, 61, 67, 68, 70, 75

International Shoe Company, 23
Intracoastal City, La., 3-5, 32
Intracoastal Waterway, 1, 3, 5, 55

Jefferson Parish, La., 8
Johnson, E. R., 81
Jones, Nelson, 42, 84
Joyce, Edward J., 81
Jungle Gardens and Bird Sanctuary, 29

Kibbe, J. E., 24, 43
King, Garfield, 21
Knapp, Frank A., Jr., 23, 75, 84
Knapp, Frank A., Sr., 23, 43, 83
Knight, Harry F., 81

LaBahn, Paul O., 81
Lafayette Parish, La., 8
Lake Charles, La., 6
Levy, A. Giffen, 7
London, England, 27
Louisiana Coast Land Company, ix, 12-23, 25, 26, 30, 31, 39, 73
Louisiana Department of State, 6
Louisiana Department of Wildlife and Fisheries, 52, 58, 59
Louisiana Furs Canal, 51, 52
Louisiana Furs Corporation, ix, x, xi, 1, 2, 14, 19, 21-24, 26, 31-34, 36, 37, 39, 40, 42-45, 55, 56, 58, 64, 69, 70, 74
Louisiana Furs, Inc., ix, xi, 1, 2, 5, 12-27, 29-34, 36, 37, 39, 40, 44, 45, 56, 57, 64, 74, 75
Louisiana Geophysical Exploration Co., 31
Louisiana Gulf Coast Club, ix, 1, 7, 8, 10, 11, 13, 14, 39, 73
Louisiana Highway 82, 4, 51
Louisiana Land and Exploration Company, 31, 32, 35
Louisiana Land and Mining Company, ix, 1, 6, 7, 10, 13, 15
Louisiana Supreme Court, 2
Louisiana Wildlife and Fisheries Commisison, 51
Louisiana Wildlife Refuge, 1
Ludlum, Anna J., 23
Luper, Oral L., 42, 84
Lyon, George A., Sr., 24, 43
Lyon, George, A., Jr., 24, 83

McBride, Lloyd M., 21, 38-41, 43, 46, 47, 50, 67, 68, 70-72, 74, 75, 80, 83
McBride, Baker, Wienke & Schlosser, 21
McBride & Baker, 21, 40, 43
McCally, J. C., 81
McCormick, Cyrus H., 81
McCrea, W. S., 82
McFadden, W. H., 7, 13, 15, 18, 20, 22, 23, 25, 31, 33, 37, 38, 82
McIlhenny, E. A., 7, 10, 12-13, 15, 22, 30, 82
McIlhenny, Edmund, Jr., 22, 75
McIlhenny, Edmund, Sr., 21, 22, 47, 50, 61, 74, 75, 83, 84
McIlhenny Company, 8, 14, 22
McIlhenny, Walter, 22, 84
Marland Oil Company, 13, 22
Marland, E. W., 13, 15, 81
Marsh Island, 45
Meehan, G. F., 17, 81
Miller, Martin O., 23, 30
Mills, W. McM., 82
Mink, 2
Moller, A. W., 81
Montague, Ken E., 84
Morton, Joy, 14-16, 25, 35, 38, 43, 81
Morton, Sterling, 19-21, 38, 43
Morton-Norwich Corporation, 21
Morton Salt Company, 14, 19, 21, 26, 33
Mulberry Canal, 4
Murray, J. C., 81

National Audubon Society, 1
National Geographic Magazine, 10
New Iberia, La., 8, 53
New Orleans, La., 15
New York, N.Y., 26
New York, N.Y., Auction Company, 27
Nikol Company, 14

Ocean Drilling and Exploration Company, 62
Orange Land Company, Ltd., 6

Paris, France, 27
Patrick, Rex. 69-71
Pecan Island, La., 4, 7, 8, 51, 52, 59
Penton, John A., 82
Perera, G. L., 82
Peterkin, Daniel, Jr., 21, 43, 74, 75, 83
Playfair, James, 82
Ponca City, Okla., 13, 22, 23
Poppenhusen, C. H., 82
Posey, E. Lloyd, 7

Index

Probasco, Scott L., Jr., 21, 22, 25, 38, 74, 84
Probasco, Scott L., Sr., 14, 20, 22, 43, 82, 83

Rainey-McIlhenny Wildlife Refuge, 1
Rand, J. O., 82
Reistle, Carl E., Jr., 42
Rip Tide Investors, Inc., 5
Rockefeller Wildlife Refuge, 1, 52
Rollover Bayou, 52

Saint Louis, Mo., 14, 17, 21-23
Schooner Bayou, 1
Schroeder Banking Corporation, 33
Sea Farm, Inc., 60
Sellers, Murphy "Red," 76, 77
Six-Mile Bayou, 3
Smith, Hubert, 69-71
Smith, Sidney, 82
Smith, Z. E., 82
Snyder and Hay, Attorneys, 12, 33, 39
Sohio Company, 53, 62
Southern Pacific Railroad, 8
Southland Royalty Company, 23, 31
Southwest Pass, 4, 46, 47
Stanolind Oil and Gas Co., 32
Steedman, Edwin H., 14-16, 21, 22, 82
Stewart, Philip B., 82
Strom, George A., 82
Swamp Land Act, 6
Tabasco Brand Pepper Sauce, 8

United States Bureau of the Budget, 49
United States Congress, 6, 50
United States Corps of Engineeers, 3-5, 45, 46, 49, 50
United States Department of Agriculture, 49, 54
United States District Court, Western District of Louisiana, 16
United States Soil Conservation Service, 54

Vermilion Bay, 1, 2, 4, 45-49
Vermilion Corporation, ix-xi
Vermilion Parish, La., 1, 3, 6, 15, 50, 51
Vermilion River, 2

Vilas, R. C., 18, 19, 82
Vilas Trust, 82

Wainwright, William III, 77
Wallace, David A "Dave," 20, 24, 38, 43, 83
Warick, W. E., 82
Washington, D. C., 47
Watkins, Horton, 23, 82
Watkins, Jabez B., 6
Westfeldt Brothers, Inc., 22
Westfeldt, George, Jr., 21, 22, 74, 84
White Lake, 1, 4
Wild Life magazine, 10
Wildlife Management Association, 50
World War II, 31
Wright, Warren, 82

Young, Edward J., 82
Young, R. O., 25-27, 30, 32, 33, 38, 76

www.ingramcontent.com/pod-product-compliance
Lightning Source LLC
Chambersburg PA
CBHW021156080526
44588CB00008B/373